C000065940

Perfect Pr

Perfect Projects

Eddie Obeng

eddie_obeng@pentaclethevbs.com

*A collection of short pieces on
exceptionally effective change
and project management ideas,
behaviours, tools and approaches*

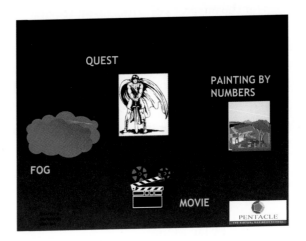

PentacleTheVBS.com/PerfectProjects.htm

First published 2003 by
Pentacle Works The Virtual Media Company
Burke Lodge
20 London End
Beaconsfield
Bucks HP9 2JH

A CIP catalogue record for this book is available from
the British Library

ISBN 095348693-1

Cover artwork by Ian Moore

Typeset by
Sparks Computer Solutions Ltd, Oxford
http://www.sparks.co.uk
Printed and bound by
Alden Press Ltd, Oxford and Northampton

For Susan

my favourite team member

Dr Eddie Obeng at Pentacle The Virtual Business School has developed a no-nonsense, anti-bureaucratic, anti-paperwork, practical approach to implementing all change. Work out who's affected, 'chunk'[1] down the change and then systematically select the best method, behaviours, team members, tools and techniques to make it happen. Eddie Obeng's *Perfect Projects* is a companion book to his *All Change!* and *Putting Strategy to Work*.

Eddie and his team of virtual tutors will coach or teach you and the key executives, managers and leaders in your organisation to embed effective change delivery in your organisation.

To find out more about the New World[2] Management Approach (NMA) and how it applies to your organisation contact Pentacle. To join other like-minded thinkers and NuvoMondists who are reinventing their enterprises visit http://PentacleTheVBS.com

---

[1] A chunk is a word for piece, like you'd break off a loaf of bread by hand or off a cold bar of chocolate.

[2] The New World referred to here is often confused with the New Economy of dot busters. It is a far bigger concept. It simply acknowledges the fact, true in most organisations, that their environment can change faster than the organisation can learn to cope with the changes. As the pace of change and complexity outstrips the rate of learning this working environment is called the New World. Organisations in this environment need leadership and management which goes beyond dealing with ambiguity to a completely New Management Approach (NMA).

Try our on-line eligibility test
(http://Pentacle.co.uk/actest.htm) and join
allchange.com – it's half price for top marks! So
read the book before you try!

PENTACLE
20 LONDON END
BEACONSFIELD
BUCKS HP9 2JH
UK
Tel: +44 1494 678 555
Fax: +44 1494 671 291
E-mail: pp@PentacleTheVBS.com
Web: http://PentacleTheVBS.com/PerfectProjects.htm

Contents

About the Author

EDDIE OBENG wants to change the world.

He has pioneered the concept of a New World of Management[3] tirelessly. His vision is to help organisations, in this post-manufacturing, post-dot-com-boom era, to create and deliver strategies which allow people to work together to their fullest potential in order to enrich their own lives and not just those of their shareholders.

Dr Obeng is Founder Director of Pentacle (1994). Previously, he was an Executive Director of Ashridge Management College, and began his career with Shell.

---

[3] New World of Management is not the same as the New Economy!

He is the author of a series of books that describe his philosophy for managing in the New World – *New Rules for the New World, All Change! The Project Leader's Secret Handbook, Putting Strategy to Work, Eddie Obeng's Money Making Machine, Making Re-engineering Happen, Soundbytes,* **Never** *Reorganise* **Again!** and *innovation: Making Dreams Live! Turning Ideas into Money.* His writing covers the full range of management topics, with lessons in fictional form and implementation techniques. Describing his books, the *Daily Telegraph* said, 'He has a backlist of book titles in a style far removed from the ponderous approach of most management tomes'. He is also a major contributor to the *Financial Times Handbook of Management* and *The Gower Handbook of Training and Development.*

In the *Financial Times* he was described as an 'agent provocateur' and a 'leading revolutionary'. *Human Resources* magazine named him as a 'rising guru.' The *Daily Telegraph* described him as the 'Max Headroom' of the business school world and 'unusual to back his own ideas with his own money'. The *Sunday Times* explained how Pentacle practises what it preaches.

Eddie regularly presents his New World philosophy, concepts and success stories to large audiences. His presentations have been described as, 'As energetic as Tom Peters but not as long ...' (*Human Resources Magazine*).

Eddie is also a regular contributor to journals, magazines and TV.

Why This Book?

I have a strange belief. I believe that most, probably **about 95%, of what happens in a project or change management initiative, is completely predictable**. When I came to this understanding one wet afternoon in October I felt compelled to write it up – to turn it into a book. The result was *All Change!* If you've read *All Change!* you'll have met Franck, my alter ego. You'll also know about the New World Management Approach (NMA) to project management. This book fills in some of the right-angled corners that *All Change!* smoothed off. If you haven't read *All Change!* read it soon. It will multiply and enhance the value of this book to you.

The title *Perfect Projects* came from a series of one-hour lunchtime workshops I ran for the BBC. The idea was that, via their hour and a half 'Learning Breaks', I was to give people a firm grounding in project leadership and change management. My initial reaction was, 'That's impossible!' You see, I believe that project leadership and management are more of a Zen-like experience, more a way of being and thinking than simply a set of tools and techniques. How do I transform people's pysche in an hour and a half? Actually, I have learnt that it is the clients who 'demand from us that which we cannot currently do' who are in fact pointing us firmly towards our own future. So I made a tremendous effort to distil weeks of project management tools, techniques, tips and behavioural hints and most importantly the 'Zen' into an hour of interaction. Then Boots the Chemists asked me for the same thing but this time they allowed me five days to complete the transformation of the psyche from line manager to Nuvo Project Leader!

I then took the idea a step further, presenting to the international project management community in Paris in 2001[1] a cyber version – 'perfectprojects@netspeed'. This time in less than an hour!

So here is *Perfect Projects*.

I've put three Trump Cards™ at the end of the book for you to cut out and use daily as reminders of the key learning points.

I've also included a list of most of the thinking, behaviours, tools and techniques my team and I have invented for your success in our New World. To find out which might be useful to you, you can try a Project Healthcheck at www.PentacleTheVBS.com/healthcheck.htm

And I've included my checklist of questions which you should constantly be asking yourself, the

---

[1] Project Leadership Conference 2001, Paris.

'Jigsaw framework' at the end of the book. I use this myself, so have a go.

And you can find more on the internet on how to make your projects perfect at http://PentacleTheVBS.com/PerfectProjects.htm. Your user name is **PP Reader** and your password is **perfect**.

The short essays on project success were related to me by Franck on a number of evenings throughout last year. I've repeated them to some of the readers of *Project Management Today* magazine. And now I'm going to tell them to you.

Perfect Projects

'What a preposterous idea! Perfect Projects! Hah! Next you'll be telling us that there is a formula for project success!'

Well actually, there **is** a formula for success and it is:

$$\left(\frac{\text{(P,C/PT*L\&R) +P\&C +SHM}}{\text{T}}\right) * \text{L} \quad = \text{Success}$$

One afternoon I had a problem. I'd been asked to re-write the brochure for my *Leading Projects Effectively* course at Ashridge Management College, and I was stuck. I'd recently inherited the course and I wasn't altogether comfortable with all the contents. I'd had one of the researchers conduct phone interviews on issues, thoughts and challenges facing project managers, and I had a huge pile of comments and statements stacked up on my desk which I hadn't analysed. I decided to apply one of my favourite research analysis tools to it. The Socratic 'bubble diagram'.[2] I got totally immersed and three hours later, without taking a single break, I had a version of the diagram that follows on the desk in front of me. But it took a further 6 months

---

[2] See *All Change*, Financial Times Publishing, 2003, Eddie Obeng – Blowing bubbles adapted from the Effect–Cause–Effect Diagram, Eli Godratt.

of study and checking to fully validate my bubble diagram. And that was when I knew I'd worked it out – the formula for project and change success.

This is the simplified version. The original version was far more complex and messy.

Read from the bottom to the top and follow the arrows without too much jumping around. Go in the same direction as the arrows and add in the words, 'If. Then ...' For example; 'If we make errors **then** we get the wrong results.'

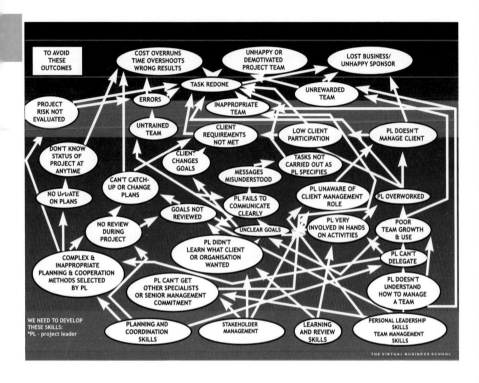

Key: PL means Project Leader

PROJECTS FAIL IN ROUGHLY THE SAME
WAYS – THERE IS A PATTERN TO THEM
GOING WRONG! IT MAY BE MESSY AND
COMPLICATED BUT THERE IS DEFINITELY A
PATTERN ...

If you want to read the diagram from the top to the bottom, use the same method, only this time go against the flow of the arrows and read the bubbles simply adding in the word 'Why?' between them. For example, The Project Leader is very involved in 'hands on activities', **Why?** because the Project Leader can't delegate.

In the original bubble diagram I tried to include and represent the different effects of what I call **the four types of change**.[3] Unfortunately, I discovered that to anyone who didn't know about or understand the four types of change, their inclusion made the bubble diagram incomprehensible. So I merged the diagrams to allow them to be comprehensible to everyone – even without an induction and explanation about change types.

What the diagram says, in summary, is that to avoid the frequently reported problems of non/late-delivery, decimated team and upset project clients there are key areas you need to focus on: **Stakeholder Management, Leadership & Team Development, Learning & Review and Planning & Coordination**. All this is set in the context of whether or not you are doing something with clear **goals and methods**.

---

[3] See later in *Why IT Projects are Doomed* – the four types are **Painting by numbers** – goal and method defined, Going on a **Quest** – goal but not method defined, Making a **Movie** – method or technology defined but not the goal and Walking through the **Fog** – neither goal or method defined.

That's where the project success formula comes from.

$$\left(\frac{(P,C/PT*L\&R) +P\&C +SHM}{T} \right) * L = Success$$

It says in English:

*Change with the right **P**urpose, matched to the right **P**roject **T**ype, kept on track through effective **L**earning and **R**eview, set up with good **P**lanning and **C**oordination plus effective **S**take**h**older **M**anagement, shared amongst the **T**eam, multiplied by (your) effective **L**eadership, equals **S**uccess.*

Projects have a definite pattern through which they fail. If you can see and understand a pattern before it occurs you can avoid it.

This is how I know that you can create Perfect Projects!

You can take our project healthcheck to see how close your project is to perfect. The healthcheck measures five dimensions of projects and scores you with a percentage. CyberFranck, our electronic coach, will also make some suggestions on what you could/should do to improve your chance of project success.

Let me know how you got on by e-mail or by logging onto allchange.com as a member.

STAKEHOLDERS

So who defines project success?

Stakeholders!

I use that question and answer to prise people away from the mechanical and Old World view that all that matters is some delivery criterion - like on time or to budget. But, if no one uses the outcome and everyone hated the experience I think it was a failure.

The first piece is a rather humorous one called Avoiding Dead Body Syndrome which I'm sure you'll recognise. The second one on Bridging The Anxiety Gap is to help you avoid those dreadful out of the blue bust-ups.

eo

Avoiding 'Dead Body Syndrome'

Technically the Project has been a tremendous success! Delivered on time, largely matching the specifications agreed at the start, and with such a small cost overshoot that you'd hardly get any change out of it if you used it to buy a Mars bar!

So why is the client refusing to buy from you again? Why has the sponsor publicly stated that they will never sponsor one of your projects again? Why have the best programmer and the best analyst in the organisation, who have just come off the team, been overheard at the coffee machine, swearing oaths at the top of their voices that they will never work with you again – and advising anyone who passes by to avoid your project leadership? Why, after such great delivery, are you finding it difficult to staff up your latest project?

This makes no sense. Time, cost and quality – the hallmarks of project quality – have been achieved and yet … The reason for this reaction is what I call 'Dead Body Syndrome'.

A real example and not a funny one:

Dead Body Syndrome I named after a client I once had (name withheld for reasons which will become obvious) who ran mining operations. I once went to visit one of their sites, a gold mine, after they

had just achieved the admirable feat of sinking a
new significantly deep shaft and finding gold! No
mean feat I assure you. And this had been achieved
to time and budget. And yet there were some real
concerns and issues on the site as we discussed the
project. They explained that they were under real
pressure to review and change many procedures
significantly. I questioned why that might be, since
the deliverables had been achieved. They explained
that because they had put so much emphasis on
delivery, and had heavily incentivised the project
leaders to deliver to time and budget, this had
pushed up their loss rate. 'Loss rate?' I inquired.
Loss rate, they explained, meant the number of
fatalities! – Hence 'Dead Body Syndrome'.

You see, it seems as if there are two ways to get a
project delivered.

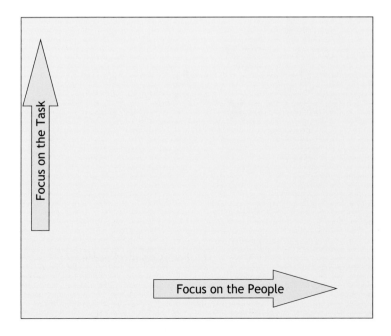

In the first you focus solely on the task – on getting the work done. You put on your big boots and kick and bully and cajole and 'influence' as hard as you can, chasing people to deliver their contributions. This way works and if you are successful and have big enough boots, the project is delivered.

Unfortunately, on the route to delivery you have stomped on so many people, ignoring the impact on them, that you have left a trail of 'dead bodies' behind you. The problem in most corporate and business projects is that these are not real dead bodies – more like zombies, because they do not just lie there waiting to be forgotten. Instead they rise up and haunt you – informing everyone of how awful it is to work with you – they lurk in

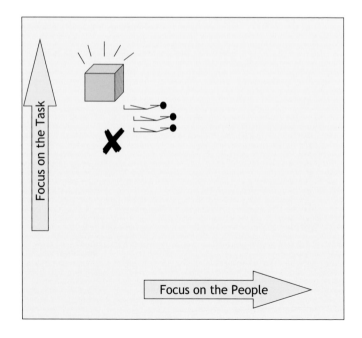

the shadows waiting for revenge or several pounds of your flesh. So as you may have now guessed, I don't recommend the big booted approach to project management.

An alternative is to focus on the people rather than the task. Build a great team, really get involvement, make sure that everyone is happy and the team and the stakeholders get on really well together. People love coming to team meetings, there are hot cookies and milk on the table, regular team building sessions down the bowling alley – along with the group learning and training session attended (note the smiling faces and happy hand holding in the diagram). Meanwhile, unfortunately, the deliverables of

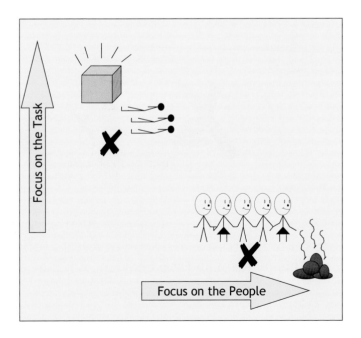

the project lie unattended, broken and neglected in the corner. No deliverables, but 'It was a great experience and I really learnt a lot!' Again, this approach does not come highly recommended from me.

A third option is to have grief and strife in the team with dead bodies strewn everywhere and the un-deliverables piled up in the corner. This I only recommend to people I don't like!

So where are we trying to get to? Well, we're trying to get to impressive deliverables AND a fulfilled and happy team and stakeholders. But how do you get there? There is little point in starting off down the dead body route, because it is impossible to transform dead bodies immediately into a happy, smiling, engaged group of stakeholders. It's almost as if there is a brick wall between the two areas. So we take the other route.

The secret is to *manage the people to manage the task*, never to manage the task directly yourself. Management by Gantt chart usually leads to chasing after tasks, rather than thinking about the people who are involved in or associated with the tasks. It is the impatience of chasing tasks out of context that often leads to dead bodies.

First, gain emotional engagement and commitment from the stakeholders and they will redirect their energy towards the task. Make sure that they understand the bigger picture and how they fit into it. Make them aware of the other people (not tasks) who are relying on them. Chase them as people, think about their competence and emotional state, challenging them to deliver their part of the shared deliverables, to play their part in the bigger picture. This way the team (and key stakeholders) become your insurance policy AND your route to deliverables (rather than the obstacles to delivery). *Manage the people to manage the task.*

Bridging the Anxiety Gap

It's been a busy week. Everything is happening all at once. After all the phoney war of the start of the project, at last you're making some progress, but not smoothly, there's still a lot to do. You need to keep the team moving, keep up the momentum on the suppliers, but instead your sponsor (or client) has just asked for a full update on project progress. It's going to take ages to put together a decent presentation and just now you haven't got the time. And when you finally do, you find that all that your update does is move your key stakeholders from very concerned to concerned. Has this ever happened to you?

I believe, and my research and experience has convinced me, that about 95% of all the things that go wrong in a project are fully predictable at the start. In the New World of business the pressures on speed, on cost and on delivering benefits make it unacceptable not to prevent all these anticipated issues before they go wrong.

So why does the scenario above occur, and why is it more prevalent in information-related and culture change/people development projects?

One of the three parameters used in defining New World projects is the visibility axis. Imagine that you are having an extension built on your house.

You get home in the evening after work. What's the first thing you do? Answer: Have a look. Of course you do, because **progress is obvious and measurable**. You are having some software written for you, you visit the programmer and ask how it's going, the programmer replies that they are almost there, but there are a few things to fix and that it will take the rest of the day. You return the next day and ask them how it's going, what do they reply? Answer: They are almost there but there are a few things to fix and that it will take the rest of the day. In this case, **progress is not obvious or easily measurable** – the first situation is what is known as a **visible project**, whilst the second is known as an **invisible project**. As a general rule the more invisible a project is the more stakeholders will demand that it is reported on.

But why does the request for the report always come at the most awkward time? The answer lies in an amazing phenomenon known as the Anxiety Gap.

Have you noticed how once a project is started, after half of the allocated time, half of the deliverables have been achieved?

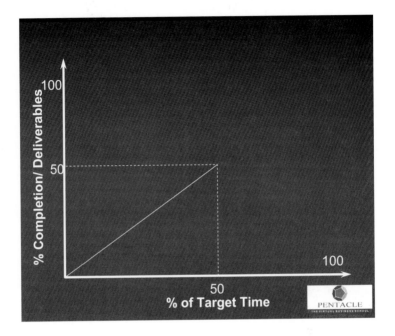

And have you noticed how this continues in a straight line, so that all the deliverables are available once the allocated time is reached?

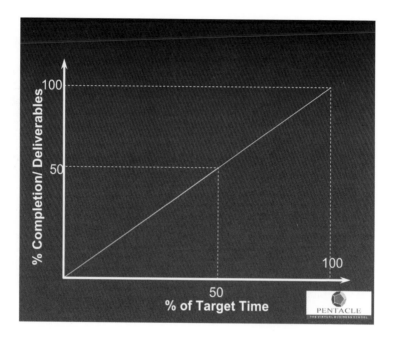

You haven't? Well, neither have I. Project progress doesn't go in a straight line, as in the previous diagrams. It tends to look more like this.

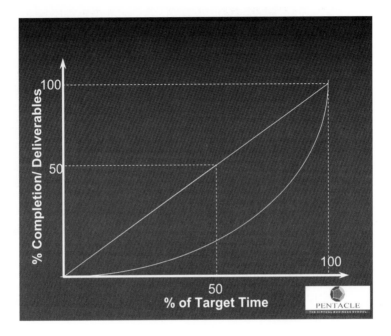

So what is happening in those early stages when there is little progress to be seen? Nothing? No! Usually those early stages are taken up with the frenetic activity of planning, building a team, gaining understanding and commitment and so on. All good things to do early in a project. Unfortunately, however, they do not necessarily produce direct deliverables.

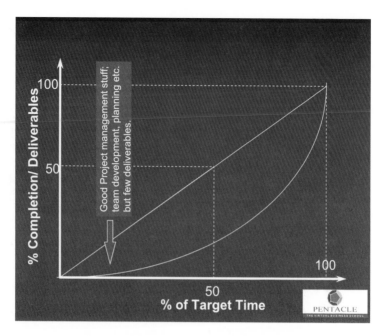

The real issue is not that we know that the progress doesn't go in a straight line. The real issue is that many other stakeholders, such as your sponsor and client, expect it to. Half the time, half the budget, they expect to see half the results.

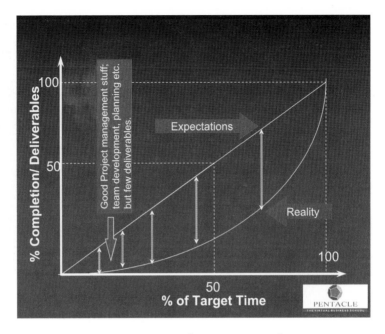

So, as you can see, a steady gap grows between their expectations and reality.

This gap is called the Anxiety Gap. This is the reason you are hauled before the executive to report on progress. This is the reason you suddenly start being asked about your projected spending.

The anxiety gap is the explanation for the scenario we began with. It is the credibility buster of many project managers. It feels wider to your stakeholders the more invisible the project is.

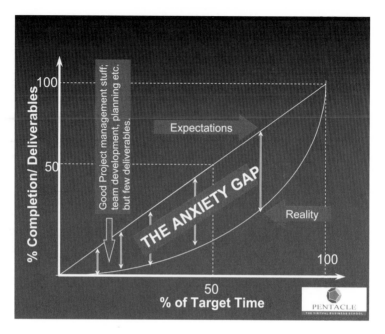

To avoid the surprise you must bridge it:

- Plan to report on activities and progress frequently.

- Develop pseudo deliverables to report on – e.g. level of team development, percentage of buy-in to concept.

- Create dummy variables or use effective communication to make the project as visible as possible.

- Warn your key stakeholders that they will experience it.

- Allocate the role of managing the gap to one of your core team.

The New World project management approach insists that you anticipate the anxiety gap and avoid its negative and time wasting effects. Remember, the best way to avoid issues in the future is to predict them ... and then fix them before they start.

CHANGE AND PROJECT TYPES

Change happens and then we either have to fix it or take advantage of it by changing something else. The 'chunk' of change we choose to do is our project! The first time I presented this idea at an international Project Management conference in Trondhiem, I split the room. Half the delegates disagreed violently and the other half agreed. It was a wonderful bun fight!

'Surviving and Thriving in a world of Change' lists my 'Laws of Change', my conclusions on how change works in the new world and some real tips on how to think and what to do.

The piece called 'Why IT projects are doomed!' is worth reading even if you aren't running an IT project. Enjoy.

eo

Surviving and Thriving in the New World of Change

Looking back a thousand years from now, historians will recognise that the late 20th century was the first time that the **pace of change** outstripped the **rate of learning** on a global scale. For those of us who are alive now, change at such a terrifying rate demands that we learn how to cope with and perhaps even manage it.

The causes of this dizzying pace are now understood – **innovation, connectedness,** the pervasiveness of **cyberspace**. In this New World of change though, there *are* some constants – one is change. Through practice and research I have discovered seven 'laws' which, if understood and applied to your thinking and behaviour, make it much easier to cope with, steer and occasionally manage change. Ignoring these laws makes failure a surprise and success elusive.

THE 1ST LAW: ONE CHANGE LEADS TO ANOTHER

Change is the seed and fruit of itself – Business strategies or tactics which fail to take into account the first law usually start off looking successful and then degenerate into failure. As a leader or manager try to anticipate the additional 'knock-on' effects of any change you start. Think through the chain of events to the end. For example, an e-mail to all staff in an organisation of 1200 people which takes 30 seconds to open will consume 10 hours of resource, costing about £1000. If your business has a margin of 10% the net result of you pressing the 'send' button is that someone will have to make an additional £10,000 of sales quickly just to stay in the same place. They may put pressure on long standing customer relations to achieve a quick result. This will probably affect customer and brand positions. Was this what you were planning?

THE 2ND LAW: ADDING CHANGE TO CHANGE CREATES 'CHAOS'

End before starting – Sometimes abandoning change = Success – Organisations are very fond of starting to implement new initiatives and strategies whilst old ones are still not complete. They will happily move a manager from one active role to another without much thought of the implications. Asking anyone at the receiving end you will easily discover that the resulting confusion often cancels out any advantage which would have been gained. Always use 'endings'

– any ritual or statement is better than none. Close or kill a major set of activities before opening another.

THE 3RD LAW: PEOPLE CREATE CHANGE - PEOPLE CONSTRAIN CHANGE

Remember the fundamental design of human beings – Imagine millions of years ago your ancestors in the primeval forest, suddenly startled by a noise. What did they do? A. Think logically about the problem? B. Start to run as fast as they could? Guess what happened to the ones who chose A? They're dead, extinct. You are here, reading this, because your ancestors chose B. Your design is: any change I observe is a potential threat to my security. This gives rise to an emotional response (usually fear, with adrenaline) and then later, when you feel safe, the logic circuits start up in your brain.

Ever met someone who has had an idea? However terrible everyone else may think it is the owner will stick to it – even calling it 'my baby'. When people invent ideas for change they often become obsessed and unstoppable in wanting the change to succeed. Create situations where people **invent** and **create** *their own* change – avoid forcing change on people, it makes them resistant.

A personal hint to make sure that you can deal with change better: Spend all your free time thinking about impossible things which do not already exist or happen in your organisation – What if we were half the size or twice the size? What if we merged with our key competitors? What if we sold our plant and leased it back? You will then have invented future change in your own mind and then when it happens you will be able to avoid an emotional reaction.

THE 4TH LAW: ACCOMPLISHED CHANGE IS CHANGE CHOSEN AND CARRIED OUT CAREFULLY

Chunk it or junk it – Choose changes which give benefits. In a business, only select change where there is a good chance that you will make more money. Good ideas, in the long run, may not allow you to survive. Break up the change and benefits into smaller pieces or projects. A grand project to install a computerised purchasing system becomes five smaller projects each with a smaller spend and earlier inflows of cash. Think about service stations. Old World: build all units – petrol station, shops, motel – and open. New World: build petrol station first, use the revenue to build the shop and eventually the motel. This way your cash flow profile looks more like a 'w' than a large deep

'V' and your exposure to the risks of your project going wrong and the risks that external events will alter the need for your project are greatly reduced.

THE 5TH LAW: THE CHALLENGE OF CREATING CHANGE IS THE CONVERSE OF THE ACCUMULATED COMPLACENCY

First we shape our organisations, thereafter they shape us – The longer people have worked in a particular way the harder it is for them to accept change. If you require easy or quick results start with people who are least entrenched in their ways. If you must fight a long history make sure that it is worth the battle.

THE 6TH LAW: RESISTANCE TO CHANGE ACCUMULATES OVER TIME AND THE CUMULATIVE NEED FOR CHANGE CAN'T BE CARRIED OUT ALL AT ONCE

Sometimes you must go backwards to go forwards – You want to create a flexible, electronic, paperless business. You may have to invent new processes which, instead of computerising, you first run with paper-based systems to get buy-in, before computerising. A single step to computerising is often just too much change and people may secretly continue with the old process.

THE 7TH LAW: SPARSELY COUPLING CHANGE CREATES CALM

Pagodas survive earthquakes – Rigid structures do not cope well with change but by loose coupling of elements of the business, networking the people, having few but clear lines of accountability in the organisation or by linking of key suppliers or customers the complexity and unpredictability of the New World can be dramatically reduced.

Problems are diverse and inexhaustible; the opportunities for change are infinite. At the same time an individual's ability is bounded and has an end. There is certainly a limit to what you can do. If you try to range over infinite change, opportunities and problems with limited resources and ability, your judgement will be biased and your spirit will end up exhausted. Remember the Laws of change and use them to Master the New World of Change and deliver Perfect Projects.

Why IT Projects are Doomed!

What do Boo.com, the National Fingerprinting Project, Taurus and the Millennium Dome have in common? Easy question – easy answer: vast overspends without the hoped-for results. But only the first three involve significant spending on IT without any real tangible result. Although you may not realise it, the odds are stacked against you if you start an information technology-based project. There are a number of very sound reasons for this.

THE RISKS AND CHANCES OF SUCCESS ARE PREDETERMINED BY CERTAIN CHARACTERISTICS

Imagine this scenario. You are buying a car. You say to the salesman, 'Well, I need to get around.' <Definition statement>. The salesman offers to study the problem and returns two weeks later with a 'driver specification' which contains sentences such as '... a circular interface will be used to orientate the appliance and the driver will be responsible for ensuring that they are fully trained in the administering of the energy source ...' <User Specification>. You are asked to put your signature to this document. How do you feel? If you don't sign it off, nothing else will happen. If you do sign it off you condemn yourself to months or years of not being able to confess that you didn't really understand, and hadn't really thought through the document you signed. <Sign-off Process>. The salesman then disappears and reappears two weeks later to inform you that his team have now worked out what they need to do. You decide to take a look at this other document, only to find the contents completely bewildering – statements like 'a minimum initial accelerator pedal compression to national speed limit not to exceed 20 seconds …' and so on <Systems/ technical specification>. To you, complete gibberish. You give up and try to hide from the salesman in order to avoid the embarrassment of being asked questions you don't even understand. The salesman persists. Every month you are brought another item to test. First the back of the seat, then the windscreen and the hubcaps <prototyping>. They all look well made, but eventually when you are presented with a green and pink Reliant Robin you realise that something must have gone wrong somewhere. You are amazed by the defensiveness which accompanies your criticisms. You are told it's your own fault – after all you signed off each stage!

An exaggerated example to make a point, but it is actually worse in reality.

Projects are 'chunks' of change we carry out to remedy, or take advantage of other changes around us. However, these chunks are not all the same. Depending on the level of learning and experience we already possess when we begin, the chunk can be 'closed'. There is no need for learning and no discussion. We understand **why** we are doing **what** we are doing, what precisely the outcome will be, and understand **how** it is to be carried out – including the methods and technologies required. In today's fast-paced new economy, my estimate is that this type of change accounts for between 10 and 30% of the change that most organisations face. Far more awkward is a climate of change with a missing method but clear goal – or a chunk of change with a clear goal or methodology but a lack of clarity on outcome – or required change which lacks both direction and method, but simply exists because 'something must be done' to get away from a real or perceived threat, or to take advantage of a real or perceived opportunity. I call these different change types, in order, **Painting by Numbers**, **Quests**, **Movies** and **Fogs**.

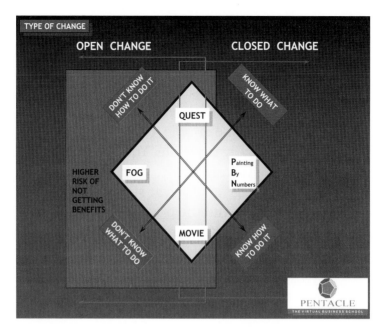

THE RISK YOU FACE IN NOT GETTING TO
YOUR GOALS DEPENDS ON WHAT TYPE OF
CHANGE YOU HAVE TO TACKLE

However, there are two other criteria which influence the chances of success. The first focuses on how easy or difficult it is to measure and monitor progress. Physical change, like construction, is highly **visible**, whilst changes to culture or, for example, to the corporate brand image are highly **invisible**. You can guess which one is going to be harder to deliver on and why. Invisible change lacks clear signals of success to those involved, and the predictability and quality of the end product is hard to determine before it is too late.

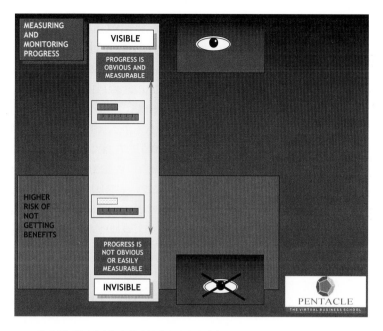

OPENNESS, VISIBILITY AND THE HUMAN
REACTIONS TO CHANGE ARE CRITICAL TO
YOUR CHANCES OF SUCCESS

The final determinant of risk and success depends on whether the party carrying out the change is the same as the party who has to live with the results. As you may have guessed, having the parties in different camps (**external** change) forces clarity on contracts and agreements. Having them in the same organisation (**internal** change) doesn't. In fact, the only situation which is more complex than internal change is Joint Venturing, where the potential for adversarial conflict associated with the external project is amplified by the internal political issues.

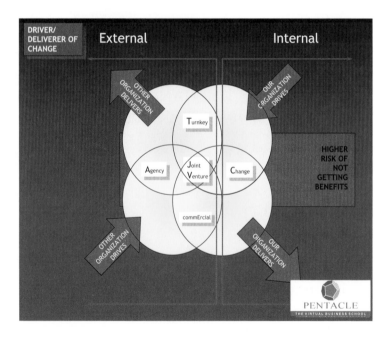

So why are IT projects doomed? Simply because they tend to fall into the more awkward and risky types; for example, the **quest** ('We must be able to have immediate access to all our enterprise information' or 'We must have client information immediately at the touch of a button'. Great, but **how** will we get there?).

Or the **movie** ('We've set up our webserver and employed 30 Java programmers to e-enable our business'. Great, but **what** will that look like?) What's even worse is that for most of the life of a technology project it remains completely **invisible**. And finally, a significant amount of this change is **internal** or abdicated **externally**.

Let me summarise this for you without the jargon. **You have a project in which some of the actual project work is going to be defining the goal, or proving the technology or method where progress is not obvious or measurable, and you can get bogged down either in internal politics or indifference or in contractual wrangling.** Now do you see why such projects are doomed?

Secondly, IT projects are doomed because the key groups of stakeholders are either unrealistic optimists or unclear 'ignoramuses'. The stakeholders who have to live with the outcomes, referred to as 'users' or 'the business', fall into the second category, whilst the leaders and team members fall into the first.

NEW TECHNOLOGY ATTRACTS OPTIMISTS AND MARGINALISES LUDDITES

Technology development in a fast changing world is bound to be difficult. It is also likely to attract people who believe in opportunities – who believe that things can work out. This is the problem. A standard team-role profiling or leadership profiling questionnaire of project leaders and team members identifies **Doers**, **Solvers**, **Checkers** and so on. But in addition, it should look for Optimists and Dreamers. To undertake something as demanding as a major IT project requires a healthy dose of optimism, but this same optimism can undermine success. Recently I met with a client who told me that when carrying out acceptance testing one box at a time, with each box taking about the same length of time to test, his team members wouldn't be even mildly concerned if after half the day, they had only made it a third of the way through the day's test goals. If asked what they thought and what they intended to do, they would reply merrily that the testing would be complete by the end of the day.

Remember, optimists always assume the best rather than communicating concerns and checking small issues.

Let me summarise the second point for you. **One group expects benefits they can't fully describe, whilst the other, the group of optimists, believe 'it will come out right' long after the early warning signals have been trumpeted.** Neither group looks hard at how this will fit in with existing practice.

The third factor is the speed of change in the New World. We all know Moore's Law, that computer power doubles every 18 months. Less well known is the fact that information velocity – the speed of information flow – is increasing by a factor of 10 every 3 years. At such a tremendous pace it is likely that any project benefits conceived will have a very short shelf-life indeed. In a piece of work I carried out with one client in the utilities industry, we discovered that any IT project which was not expected to deliver results within the first 18 months never paid back at all! The problem is that projects are chunks of change we carry out to take advantage of new opportunities to fix issues in our existing enterprises. There are two components: effort and benefits. In most project schedules the project is defined as the effort – the work to be done to establish the change. The benefits are not defined as part of the project. It is assumed that somehow they will take care of themselves.

Getting benefits early -

Effort followed by reward
'V' strategy

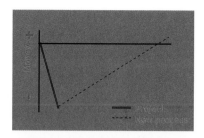

Effort and reward interleaved
'w' strategy

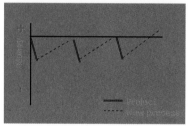

From *All Change! The Project Leader's Secret Handbook,*
Dr Eddie Obeng, available at allchange.com, Copyright Obeng 2000

CHUNK IT OR JUNK IT!

The people who have to change their work habits, develop their skills, etc. will just get on with it and all will be well. As a result, the people who actually have to change what they do on a day-to-day basis are rarely seen as the key stakeholders in the project. In addition, projects often ignore the dismantling of the pre-existing systems and infrastructure, which is often essential to encourage the changes required to reap the benefits.

Also, projects often fail to be effectively chunked. If broken down at all, the breakdown is by effort not by benefit. It is more common to complete the development of a complete platform before adding applications, than to specify the platform and construct enough for the deployment of an early application.

In summary – **The purpose of the project, and the technologies contained in it, will get out of date so fast that it is easy to deliver a project which does nothing but present the enterprise with a huge bill with little obvious means of recouping the costs.** Organisations who recently implemented enterprise-wide accounting and reporting systems, which are now being upgraded to be web browseable, will recognise this effect.

WHAT TO DO ABOUT IT?

Even the more apparently risky open projects
can be successfully delivered if the right method
is applied. For example, instead of applying a
'Method One' style painting-by-numbers approach
to a more open quest …

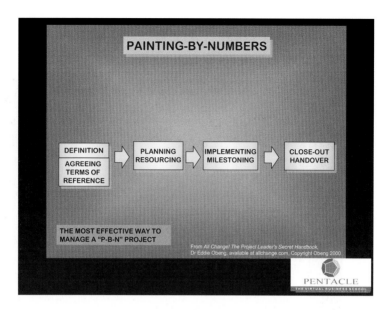

THERE IS A SINGLE BEST APPROACH FOR MANAGING EACH TYPE OF PROJECT.

Painting by Numbers goes linearly and sequentially

… for going on a quest a parallel track approach (similar to RAD) should instead be applied.

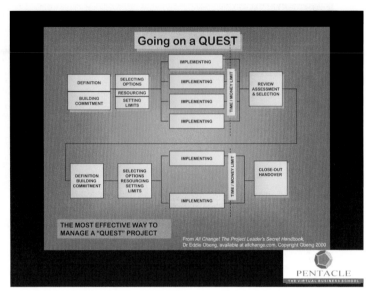

THERE IS A SINGLE BEST APPROACH FOR MANAGING EACH TYPE OF PROJECT.

Quests work in parallel and converge

Deadlines should be close and immovable.

In addition, anything and everything which can be used to raise the visibility of the project should be done. Mock-ups, prototypes, review presentations, stakeholder simulations, should be applied liberally as an integral part of the project.

… for making a movie

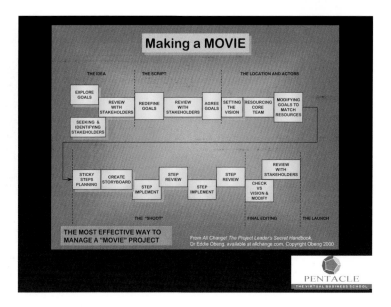

THERE IS A SINGLE BEST APPROACH FOR
MANAGING EACH TYPE OF PROJECT.

A movie checks and clarifies before moving on

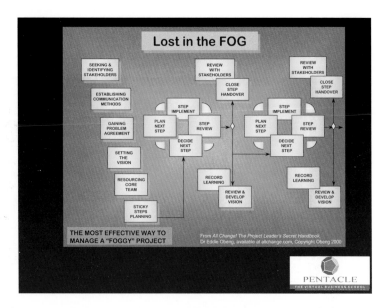

THERE IS A SINGLE BEST APPROACH FOR
MANAGING EACH TYPE OF PROJECT.

Fog goes in circles - with a strict drum beat!

The stakeholder management is also critical – the
user stakeholders must be encouraged to fully
understand what is going to change, and what is
going to stay the same, as a result of the project.
Again, simulations, 'a day in the future of …'-type
exercises and communication using the user's
journey rather than the developer's specification
are critical. The other stakeholders, the team and
leaders need constant reviews and checkpoints and
a healthy dose of self criticism and cynicism, to
ensure that risks and early warning signs are not
ignored.

THE COMPLETE PROJECT LOOKS BEYOND THE EFFORT OR THE BENEFITS AND TAKES ALL INTO ACCOUNT IN ITS PLANNING AND IMPLEMENTATION

It is important to plan on the basis of **'the complete business project'** – that is, <u>all</u> the people and activities which have to be coordinated through change to give the overall business benefit. Projects should be phased not by technical requirements but instead by the efforts/rewards – that is, the flow of money to be 'w' shaped rather than 'V' shaped or in the case of complete failures, 'L' shaped.

So perhaps not all IT projects are doomed! At least not the ones who apply the clear lessons of past failures.

LEADERSHIP AND TEAM DEVELOPMENT

Project teams have become more complex. Not only do you have to deal with people who report to you but also with people in other parts of the organisation and even in other organisations! And there's no time to really get to know the people you work with. Sometimes you have to get them working together fast. The three pieces I've selected deal with the challenges we face. Leaders! Who needs them? helps you to work out how to change your behaviour to gain more effective leadership. Together Everyone Achieves More! is my shortcut to team performance, and Consultants ... Always ride them like a horse! should save your organisation a fortune! Remember, behaviour is where the rubber hits the road.

Leaders! Who Needs Them?

You're on a training course – an experiential training course. One of those courses where the tutor sets up an exercise, something like one of those ranking exercises – you're lost in the desert – stuck in the arctic – crashed on the moon. You and eleven other colleagues have to put in correct order 20 random objects. You have 30 minutes.

A week later – it feels like a week, but it's only 45 minutes later – you are suffering the acute embarrassment of watching yourselves on the play-back of the CCTV video. It's a shambles and there is real evidence. What went wrong?

Now the tutor is waffling on some stuff about leadership and how, by not being clear on your roles and accountabilities, and by not having a leader to help to define the goal, you have gone off track.

One member of your group comments that you are all colleagues and so it would not feel right to have someone bossing the rest of you about.

The tutor is trying to explain some semantic difference between a boss or manager and a leader, but you are lost in your own thoughts. You are thinking leadership is bunk. At work, in the real world, the project manager simply manages. The methodology you use provides the project manager with a steering committee and a project board of very senior people, which takes all the decisions and makes sure that everyone does what they are supposed to, period.

Anyway, only last month your organisation's best project manager was fired for doing this leadership stuff. For the past three years they had been responsible for a series of expansion projects, opening a series of new offices and branches across Europe. Nine months ago they were given a smallish project on 'web-enabling' the organisation. This was seen as their 'opportunity to demonstrate leadership qualities'. Nine months later, six key staff had quit complaining of 'bullying' and 'a lack of creativity and lack of opportunity to explore the issues'. On top of that, the consultants who put the detailed implementation plan together had left the company £250K richer.

No, you're not convinced. Anyway, you read somewhere that leaders are born that way. So you are either a leader or you're not. Fortunately the tutor has stopped talking and it's time for your coffee break.

Leaders! Who needs them? Well, actually, we do if we are carrying out 'Big Change', change involving several other people in an organisation in this ever-changing New World.

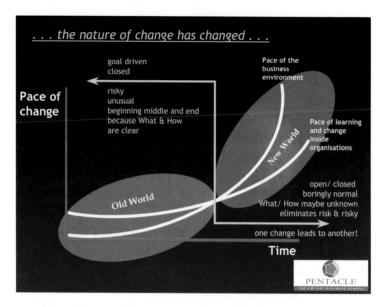

In the Old World most organisations could learn and adapt faster than the world was changing. Change tended to be an unusual and discrete set of events.

Most of the business' activity was focused on maintaining and delivering more of the same. The net result was that we built organisations which were compartmentalised in simple hierarchical structures, with the most experienced people at the top controlling the actions of all those below, through a linear command and control system. When a change was required it was common to be clear on **what** was to be achieved (Outcome) and **how** it was to be done (Method/Technology).

The way in which the project was set up mirrored the way the organisation was set up. The project organisation was made up of representatives from the organisation, with the project leader as the boss and a steering group or F.O.G. (otherwise known as Friends Of God) to keep the project manager on the straight and narrow.

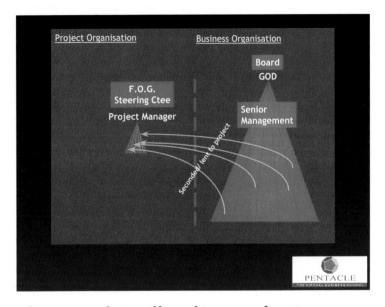

This approach is still used in several project management methodologies today. However, the world has altered. The pace of change can outstrip our ability to learn and change. **In several projects we are unsure of the *what* or the *how* or both!** The ability of the members of the F.O.G. to really understand, and therefore take the right decisions on behalf of the whole organisation, is severely diminished – sometimes the expertise and knowledge lies well below the senior levels.

In addition, the organisation is complex and geographically spread, and their ability to impose their will on all the people affected by the change is severely reduced. People can appear to be complying whilst actually resisting the change. Many of the changes introduced are unfamiliar, and cause people to react to them emotionally rather than entirely logically. In short, there are many stakeholders throughout the organisation, all of whom need to be aligned if the project is to deliver the benefits sought. There are stakeholders who help the project and those who have to live with its results. Some will alter their own personal behaviour and carry out actions to make sure that the benefits can be reaped. Finally, in most modern organisations, there are a whole host of projects required, and it is unlikely that there will be enough 'most senior' people to manage them. This means that most project managers will have to move, emotionally engage and influence stakeholders who are senior to them. These stakeholders will be in other functions/ departments of the businesses. These stakeholders they cannot **manage**.

This is when **leadership** starts to be relevant. Because *you can only manage people you have authority over, but you can lead anyone*. Think of a good movie you have been to lately. The director isn't your boss but somehow they make you behave a certain way – sit in the cinema for almost two hours following the twists and turns of their plot. (In a bad movie you walk out/daydream, etc.)

So what is the difference between management and leadership? Is there one?

How did you become a manager? I guess for most people, they hang about in the organisation. Eventually another manager approaches them, taps them on the head and says 'Thou art now a Manager. Arise and take your car keys.' And they become a manager. In other words, **other managers** make **you** a manager.

How do you become a leader? Do other leaders make you one? Do you decide that you are one and then you become one?

Two short scenarios.

(a)   One of your colleagues turns up for work wearing a bright blue and orange suit with shoes to match. The next week, a dozen more of your colleagues turn up for work dressed exactly the same way.

(b)   One of your colleagues turns up for work wearing a bright blue and orange suit, and spends all day telling everyone that this is the height of fashion. Everyone laughs and no one is ever seen wearing anything even remotely as ridiculous.

Strange, but it is the action of **other people** deciding to follow you that makes **you** a leader.

But what exactly makes people follow? In the Old World people would follow you because of your position in the organisation, status, birthright, or simply because you were the only game in town. The New World has made this more complex. In many organisations employees are empowered, which means that they get a say in who they decide to follow.

So how do you make them follow you? The secret is, that people follow a leader's behaviour far more than what they say or where they sit. In the New World a leader (you) goes into their world and works out how they would like to be led, and then thinks about the actual situation, and selects behaviours which are more likely to magnetise them in any situation.

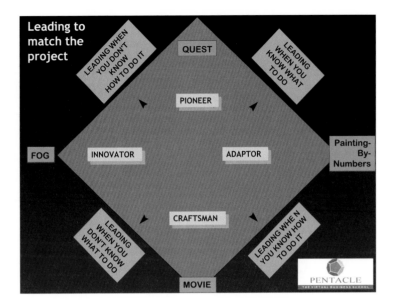

Leading to match the project

QUEST

LEADING WHEN YOU DON'T KNOW HOW TO DO IT

LEADING WHEN YOU KNOW WHAT TO DO

PIONEER

FOG

INNOVATOR

ADAPTOR

Painting-By-Numbers

CRAFTSMAN

LEADING WHEN YOU DON'T KNOW WHAT TO DO

LEADING WHEN YOU KNOW HOW TO DO IT

MOVIE

PENTACLE
THE VIRTUAL BUSINESS SCHOOL

ADAPTOR

Know and understand the methods and techniques employed in the project

Clearly define goals

Clearly communicate the goals to all the groups of specialists involved in the project

Set challenging standards

Assign tasks to team members

Define the boundaries between the tasks

Resolve conflicts and boundary issues

Be firm but fair in dealing with team members

Organise their own time

Plan activities for the whole project

Separate the essential many tasks from the critical few

Select the key skills and the behaviours required of the project

Identify corrective actions if the progress starts to deviate from the plan

Offer motivation through reward and punishment

Manage handover of deliverables

Prevent stakeholders external to the project from directly interfering with the project

PIONEER

Encapsulate the solution to the problem in a persuasive vision

Communicate the vision enthusiastically

Gain personal ownership for the idea from the team

Select team members capable of pursuing the challenge

Live the values embodied in the project

Offer motivation through 'fame and fortune' opportunities

Must be single minded (almost to the point of obstinacy)

Keen and willing to try methods which the leader does not fully understand in order to achieve the goal

Set limits to each line of enquiry on the basis of time or resources (financial or non-financial) called check points

Strictly and fairly enforce the limits to each line of enquiry

Monitor progress and eliminate unfruitful searches

Encourage sharing of learning across the team

Maintain the vision and its seductiveness in the light of short term failure

Demonstrate courage & show genuine concern for team members

CRAFTSMAN

Be persistent in defining the goals of the project - including active listening

Hold a steady vision in his/her head for long periods of time

Be more interested in the goal of the project than in the use of the method or technology

Be almost obsessive about high quality standards

Find opportunities for team members to use their skills to the fullest

Set challenging personal visions for team members

Demonstrate experience or understanding of the main technology or methodology used

Build a vision of the project goals from stakeholder aspirations

Keep the use of the methodology as far in the background as possible without demotivating the team

Be able to speak the language of the team specialists

Review progress against the vision

Continuously review quality and not move on until the deliverables meet the quality objectives of the vision

Be able to raise the visibility of the vision among the team

Make sure that the team all understand how their role contributes to achieving it

Prevent the team from delivering results not in line with the vision

Provide space for creativity in line with the vision

Demonstrate aspects of the vision

Motivate through relationships & appear to know all the team personally

INNOVATOR

Build trust - Make promises and keep them

Find a wide range of stakeholders many of whom do not initially see themselves as stakeholders

Be prepared to go to where the team are, logically and emotionally (match and lead)

Communicate widely and use questions effectively

Listen effectively to both logical and emotional concerns

Demonstrate calmness (even when panicking)

Describe and capture the nature of the problem faced

Clearly articulate a vision (usually the opposite of the problem faced)

Show genuine concern for the team

Keep stakeholders informed on a day-to-day basis

Encourage the team to communicate amongst themselves

Capture any learning the team makes - Proceed one step at a time

Reassure team members - Be creative with any new opportunities or insights which present themselves

Give hope to the stakeholders - Praise initiative taken by the team

Provide intellectual challenge through questioning and problem description

Analyse complex situations and distil the few actions likely to give the biggest results

Accept offers of ideas and efforts from the team

Involve team in decision making & provide a stable 'base'

Selecting the wrong behaviour in each situation is likely to lead to failure. Someone who had led several **'Painting-by-Numbers'** type projects, would probably have created a set of habits and behaviours for leading people in that situation. When presented with a **'Lost in the Fog'** type of project, such as web-enabling the organisation, the same structured, ordered and directive behaviours that work in the 'Painting-by-Numbers' situation, are completely inappropriate.

Now are you convinced? You can see how leadership works on anyone, how it works, how it can be learnt and when different behaviours should be applied. Maybe that tutor wasn't talking such hot air after all.

Leaders. Not only do we need them – but we also need **you** to be the right one for the type of project.

Together Everyone Achieves More!

What a meeting! Team huh! When it works it's the best feeling in the world. When a team comes together it's a real buzz. People looking out for each other, no challenge too great. But this team … I just don't know, a couple of them just don't want to be here … and when we have team meetings, it's like they're all running different agendas. I mean, look at that dialogue between Janet and John, it was a reasonable suggestion, John didn't need to snap so aggressively!

The problem isn't that teams just don't work. It's that teams don't just work.

In the New World of business we form and reform teams continuously – most of us belong to several teams at any time. But if you're like me, you're happier working in some teams than others. And if you're like me, you often have the challenge of being the leader and trying to make the team work.

A GROUP OF PEOPLE ISN'T NECESSARILY A TEAM

A few years ago, I visited an organisation which had recently introduced a personal accountability and performance incentives package for its staff. It was a great package created and designed by a group of the world's leading human resources consultants – so what was the problem? The problem was that team working in the functions, which had already been fragile and faltering, completely collapsed. Of course it did. In most business functions, people are working in the same department but doing parallel jobs – they have similar/parallel goals, but if you think about it, I can get promoted for hitting my sales target whilst you get no bonus at all. What we need, and don't have, is a **COMMON GOAL**.

A BUS QUEUE HAS A COMMON GOAL BUT IT ISN'T A TEAM

So would it be OK if we had a common goal? Well no, it's not enough. You see, outside my window at work there is a bus stop and I often see people queuing for a bus. I think, 'Ah! group of people with a common goal – that must be a team!' Of course it's not, because the second ingredient is missing. What each and every member of a team needs to believe is that they can't succeed on their own. And even more important, they need to recognise that no one else can succeed alone. So not only am I dependent on you, you are also dependent on me. We are **INTERDEPENDENT**.

People in a bus queue are not interdependent.

MUTUAL ASSURED DESTRUCTION ISN'T A RECIPE FOR TEAMWORK

So would it be enough simply to give everyone a common goal, and then to make them interdependent by say, giving them a team bonus so that we all succeed or fail together? Well no, that's not enough either. I came across an organisation which slashed the salaries of their sales people and instead, put them on a shared bonus scheme. Net result – finger pointing and blame, followed by blood on the carpet, the departure of the best sales person and missed targets. How could this happen? It happens because before you become interdependent with anyone else, you need to be absolutely sure that they won't drag you down with them – you have to believe that they can provide a **PERSONAL CONTRIBUTION**. Something to help you and the rest of the team.

So for an effective team to form, someone – perhaps the leader – needs to make sure that the people in the group want to be **included** in the group (this is why a good leader, when putting together a team, will sell the attributes of the team members to each other). And then someone needs to make sure that people feel that they have enough **control** over what's going on (this is why in the early stages of forming a team, a good leader will speak up for the people less willing to take control, and will try to take control from the more dominant individuals). And then someone needs to make sure that people see each other as human beings, and can share task-related and personal concerns **openly.** (Which is why a good leader will share personal views openly, and encourage others to do the same.) Increased openness often makes people feel more comfortable about being included, and less worried about controlling what is happening, allowing them to relax and be more open and supportive and so closing the **CIRCLE OF INCLUSION**™.

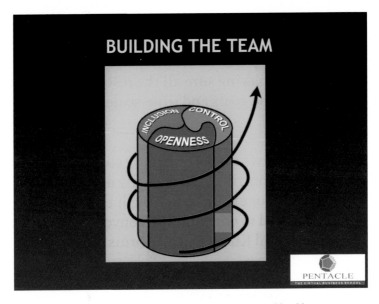

So, creating the circle of inclusion will allow people to contribute, and then teaming should all go smoothly.

PEOPLE TRYING TO CONTRIBUTE CAN BE THE MAIN CAUSE OF TENSIONS IN THE TEAM

Well not quite – you see, different people feel that they contribute different things to a team. Some people believe that they add value to a team through the knowledge and expertise they bring to the team (**Knowers**). Others think the team values them for their ideas and suggestions (**Solvers**). Others think it is their ability to make the team a great place to work (**Carers**). Or they feel that they act as the backbone of the team by making sure that the work gets done (**Doers**). And a final group thinks of themselves as the quality assurers, making sure all the resources are used and realistic goals and time-scales are pursued (**Checkers**).

The bad news is that, in trying so hard to really help, the contributions actually don't sit well together. For example, although they are both trying hard to contribute, a conversation between a Solver and Knower can be bruising ...

<Solver> Why don't we try ...

<Knower> It's not done that way!

Or try this one.

<Carer> I'm not sure everyone is happy about that.

<Doer> I don't care. We need to get on!

But the final twist in the tale is that these team contributions are **not all equally valid** on the four different types of project.

Imagine a Painting-by-Numbers project with a team made up entirely of Solvers. What a nightmare! All the effort would be spent in reinventing the project rather than delivering it. A Foggy project with a team of Knowers will deliver a solution not related to the problem which they faced, but a solution that had been used before!

So there you go now! All team problems solved.

No, not really. Most project managers have little or no say in who actually joins their teams.

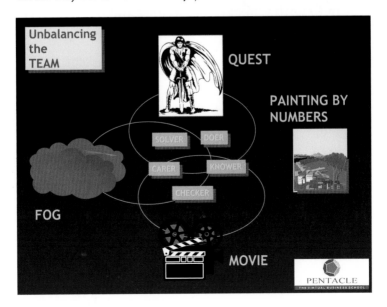

Also, there may be specific skills, competences or abilities which are crucial to the content of the project. There will be personal 'history' and rivalries to account for, and you may be forced to have participation from specific departments or functions.

In your world and mine, the best we can do is to understand the impact of ensuring that there is a common goal, interdependence and that people can make personal contributions. We can have up-our-sleeves strategies and tactics to cope with missing behaviours. For example, you may want to add additional brainstorming sessions to account for a lack of Solver behaviour, training or visits from experts to up the Knower behaviour, working meetings and tight time-scales to encourage Doing, formal sign-offs and client review to help with Checker behaviour and to cope with a shortage of Carer behaviour – you will go bowling!

So spend time thinking about your team and their contributions, and think how you will compensate for missing behaviours.

Consultants ... Always Ride Them Like a Horse!

You've lost control. The budget figures you are looking at on the screen of your laptop are all in red. Deep red. You call a meeting of all the key stakeholders and team members, but when you try to speak, your jaws are wired shut and instead, the consultant you are using, stands up to lead and chair the meeting. You listen in horror as the scope of the project expands to include almost every fashionable management fad, balanced scorecards, CRM, e-enablement ... The external suppliers you have been working with are grinning from ear to ear, pound notes flutter from the ceiling and form a large but neat pile in front of them. All the while, your joint venture partner is repeating the mantra, 'Effort is yours – Benefit is mine'.

It's only a dream, a nightmare, but you still wake with a start and feel unsettled enough to make the long journey downstairs to the fridge for a glass of cold water.

As the New World continues to take a hold of the real world, more and more projects become virtual. They cut across the organisation, across a number of strategic or non-strategic partner organisations, across an increasing range of suppliers, across countries, continents and across the time-zones of the globe. This environment is fertile opportunity for professionals who specialise in advising organisations in complex situations – consultants.

Traditionally, the role that most consultants had on projects was to act as 'transferors of knowledge or best practice' – people who had seen a situation or solution elsewhere, and could be relied upon to provide that solution to the client. Or had a killer methodology to apply. However, there is a fundamental problem. One of the key things which defines the New World of business is the fact that change occurs faster than we can learn – so a problem which is genuinely new to the client, is also probably genuinely new to the consultant. Or worse, a problem that looks familiar to the consultant, may actually rely on a completely new solution for the client. So what value does the consultant bring?

Even worse, is the issue of misaligned goals. We all know that a team only becomes a team if three specific conditions are available: a common, shared or aligned goal or objective, a belief in interdependence (this means the members of the team recognise that they cannot succeed without each other), and an acceptance of personal accountability and contribution. This is where the most intractable problem lies with using consultants.

Any decent consultancy operation is confident. The consultants are confident (and occasionally arrogant) that they can solve the client's problems, even though they may never have set foot in the client's organisation or industry before. Any decent consultancy operation is highly profitable. Profitability is achieved by selling the time of a high-quality consultant. However, the problem is that if you don't sell Today today, you can't sell Today tomorrow (any time missed out on cannot be later resold). Another problem is that you can only sell one person's time once. So for a consultancy to make money, it uses two amplifiers. Firstly it tries to make sure that somebody is paying (as much as possible) for every second of the day – this is known as rate realisation. Furthermore, it tries to make sure that the work is passed down (to as junior a person as possible) to create opportunities for selling time at the highest possible rate – this is called leverage. This business model is the source of misalignment. Your consultant may believe that they can do a better job than you, the project leader, and worse, the more time they can sell you at the highest rate whilst stuffing the project with the most junior and inexperienced person they can find, the better the job they are seen to be doing, and the more successful they are <u>in their own organisation</u>. (I know all this from personal experience as an ex-consultant now turned business educator.) As a project leader this is not what you want. However, it is a fact of life and so you need to deal with it.

The first questions I recommend you ask are 'What am I using consultants for?' 'Why do I need them?'

The simple four-box matrix below is a way of thinking about what the consultant brings to the project. I've used a medical analogy to make it more easily understood.

Role played by consultant

	Help/Support	Solutions
Expert	Psychiatrist	Surgeon
Generalist	Nurse	GP

Select the box you feel the consultant fits into, and then define the success criteria, 'I will know I have had value from the consultant when ...' For example, a 'Nurse'-type consultant is part of the project in order to provide resources and support – don't look to them for solutions, and make sure that they are clear that that is not their role. And remember, usually 'Surgeons' cost more than 'Nurses', and also 'Surgeons' usually take all their knowledge and experience away with them. So, in the New World, where you want your organisation to learn faster, if you want real knowledge transfer from 'Surgeons' or 'Psychiatrists', you'll have to provide good people (housemen/understudies) to shadow and learn from them and set up processes to ensure knowledge retention.

Don't forget to gross up your consultant's fees by a factor of 5, to get a feel for the revenue you will have to generate to cover the cost of their contribution.

As I mentioned, be aware that most consultants charge for their time and that they have targets to meet, so in general they try to sell you the longest contribution they can think of, rather than the one which is going to be most effective for the project. This means that they will often sell initially in an area of competence where they really help you, but unfortunately they may keep selling you time until their contribution is of little value. *So, be wary about carrying out the last phase that they suggest. It is likely to be at the lowest cost/benefit ratio.*

This means that **the honesty, integrity and personal values of the consultant are critical factors to take into consideration.** There are a fair proportion of consultants who, in-spite of all the drivers and reasons I have described above, will only have your very best interests at heart. These consultants once found should be cherished. They will advise you on when it is better to get help from someone else. Look for organisations who are more interested in the quality of their work and the relationship, than on increasing size and growing their number of consultants – also it helps if they are near to or at capacity – since they then try to do the most effective job as quickly as possible to free up resources. *So don't forget to ask them how busy they are.*

Work with your consultants. Be sure to **set hard and soft success criteria for them**, and agree clear ground rules and performance levels. Decide the extent to which they form a part of the core team, and never, even with the good ones, trust them not to try to take over the leadership of the project.

The secret is to **'ride them like a horse'.** Establish leadership. Set the length of the reins. Feed them apples and get them to keep the speed and pace of deliverables up – with a sharp kick! The only thing that doesn't fit into the analogy is that you aren't allowed to use the whip!

PLANNING AND COORDINATION

Eddie Izzard once made me laugh uncontrollably with his 'of mice and men' sketch where he asks 'best laid plans of mice? Who ever heard of mice making plans?' The pity is that there are also some men who never make plans - even on complicated ventures ... I have for you three pieces here. The first, In the Fog, first focus and then move forward one step at a time, is my description of two of the most powerful tools I teach, Gap Analysis^{TM} and the famous Sticky Steps^{TM} method which has been described as 'taking the terror out of planning'.

Is your project organisation a tangled web? is an explanation of how my OrganoWeb, normally used to replace the hierarchy in organisations, can be applied specifically to projects. There is a short piece on The project leader's decision making process at the end of this section.

In the Fog, First Focus and then Move Forward One Step at a Time!

Your eyes feel full of grit. And so they should. Three hours' sleep on a Thursday night after a tough week isn't enough for anybody – not even you. Three hours' sleep. Four hours spent worrying. It started with *'Something must be done about our level of innovation. And it must be done urgently. We are not growing as fast as the market place. You are going to deliver and I need a detailed plan and business case by Monday.'* Fatal words, uttered by your VP. You respond, demanding a clearer brief. His response, 'If you can't deliver can you suggest someone else who can?' Stalemate. Where to start? Who to include? What to do? How to estimate the costs? How to scope it? How even to write a business case? Aargh! If only you had a better brief. You've tried to create a Gantt chart and got stuck. You don't have enough information for a critical path analysis and you definitely can't do any present value calculations.

When your organisation asks you to deliver a project different from any that have been done in the organisation before, a project where the **goals are unclear** and **how to** achieve them are **unclear** (and often no one even understands why it needs to be done) you will find yourself walking through what I call a thick FOG. These days **'Foggy projects'** (as opposed to Painting-by-Numbers projects) are more and more common (along with the other two types, Quests and Movies[4]). Foggy projects are hard to get a handle on and they engage your emotions. So does that mean that if you end up leading a Foggy project you are doomed?

No. I believe not.

Today, as a project leader, you need to have the skills and capabilities to manage **all change**, however open and uncertain. You need to use different tools and techniques from the ones you learnt on your MBA or Prince II course. You need techniques and tools invented specifically for the New World.

So you don't know what the project is? So you can't plan it? No problem! Working on your own you could create a Bubble Diagram[TM] (See *All Change!* FT Publishing). But if you are working with others I would recommend you go for a Gap Analysis[TM] – not as precise as a bubble diagram – but it allows everyone, all your stakeholders, to become emotionally engaged and share the ownership of both the problem and the solution. The most powerful way to use these tools is in

[4] See *Project Manager Today* magazine, April 2002.

combination with another of my inventions, Sticky Steps^{TM}.

In Foggy project situations, however, it's very rare that the first problem people settle on is the actual problem they face.

You need a flip chart and a 'wodge' of post-it notes. Lay out your flip chart as I've drawn it below.

...IF NOT FIXED...	... IF FIXED...

< GAP >

WHY NOT FIXED YET?
(POSSIBLE CAUSES)

PENTACLE
THE VIRTUAL BUSINESS SCHOOL

Now choose your sentence. This is your gap. This gap is the first thing you write down on a post-it. Stick it slap-bang in the middle of your flip chart workspace.

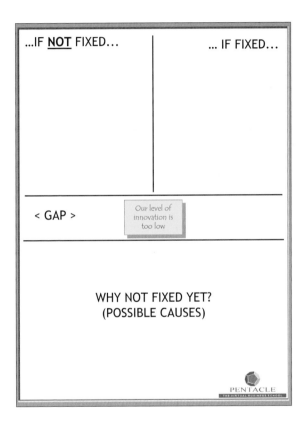

You've been losing sleep because, *'Something must be done about our low level of innovation'* And that is how you start a Gap Analysis^{TM}. There is obviously a difference, **a gap** between the current state of affairs and the desired state of affairs. How would you describe this gap? See if you can find a sentence to describe it. Involve other people in the discussion. You'll probably discover that there are three or four sentences which describe the gap between the current state and the desired state. Work on them one at a time. In this case you could start with the sentence you got straight from your VP. *'Our levels of innovation are too low'* and *'We are not growing as fast as the market place.'*

Now you've got to work out if the gap is worth closing.

Workshop this. Hand out the pads of post-its. The first question you and your group must answer is, **'What will happen IF this gap is <u>NOT</u> FIXED?'** Ask each participant to write out a post-it each with their strongest view. Everyone gets the same number of 'votes' (two/three post-its if your group consists of less than ten people). Encourage them to quantify the effects if possible – cost overall, cost per year, etc.

Gather up the post-its and group them on the flip chart. Arrange the groups so that they tell a story as you read them out loud going upward and away from the gap. **'This is our gap. If we don't fix it ...'**

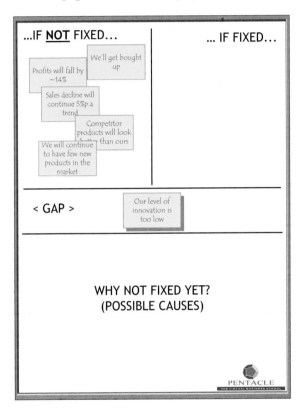

Now ask them to write a post-it each about what they anticipate will happen if the Gap is closed, **IF FIXED**, and repeat the step above.

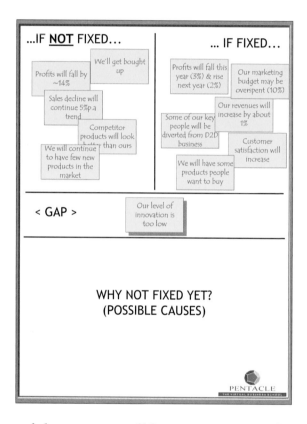

Some of the post-its will have comments which are the opposite of the ones on what happens if it's not fixed. That's fine but encourage the participants to think more widely, and also to quantify the effects wherever possible.

Now a quick pause for reflection. You have the full 'do nothing' story as well as the benefits/outcomes story. In other words you have the **basis of your business case**.

In Foggy project situations, however, it's very rare that the first problem people settle on is the actual problem they face. To try to get a bit deeper below the surface we return to the Gap, but this time we try to work out **why** the gap actually exists – '**Why hasn't the gap been fixed yet?**'

Again, cluster the results by similar comments and then try to group them so that they tell a story as you read them from the bottom up.

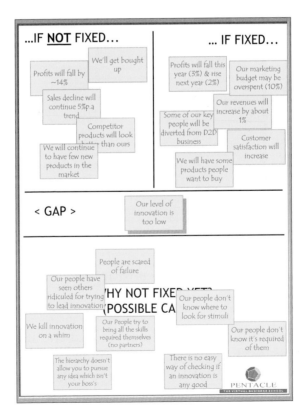

So you now have a few clusters of things which are stopping the gap from being closed. I call these cluster topics **'anchors'**. All these issues need to be included in the scope of the project if it is to succeed.

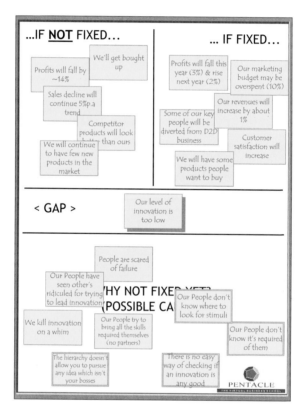

This is achieved using post-its and 'voting' as before.

In addition, you will discover that the anchors contain the names or departments of many of the people who are likely to be key stakeholders.

So now we have some clues about 'Where to start? Who to include? How to scope it? How even, to write a business case?'

MAKING PROGRESS THROUGH THE FOG - ONE 'STICKY STEP' AT A TIME

In a Foggy project, *starting is more important than making absolutely sure you know where to start and everything about the project before you start.* But I always recommend that, to manage the risk and also improve the learning and chances of success, you establish a project 'drumbeat'. This drumbeat is the frequency with which you will re-plan and review to check that you are getting closer to a solution.

So let's plan how we are going to eliminate one of the cluster anchors we've identified. For this we use Sticky Steps™. The Sticky Steps™ process works like planning in reverse. We pretend we've succeeded with the project and then we brainstorm how we succeeded in a strict format around a simple sentence. **In order to have ... we must have ...**

So starting with the cluster which said, *'There is no easy way of checking if an innovation is any good,'* we rephrase that as its 'opposite', as a goal. Perhaps as *'Created an easy way of checking if an innovation is any good.'*

Sticky Steps™ is a structured brainstorm in which you simply dream up endings for a sentence. Read the sentence out loud.

IN ORDER TO HAVE ... (VERB) ....　　‹WHAT?›

WE MUST HAVE...(VERB) ....

PENTACLE
THE VIRTUAL BUSINESS SCHOOL

Fill in the 'What?' using one of your cluster anchors.

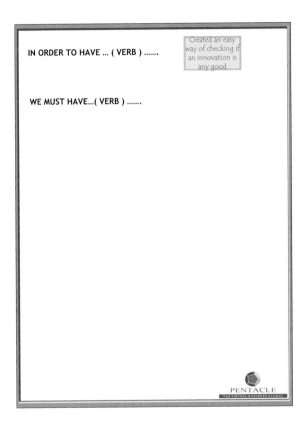

So let's just complete the sentence – no wild guesses which don't fit the sentence are allowed. Our problem now becomes that we have five more Foggyish things to deal with. No problem, we'll just repeat the process again.

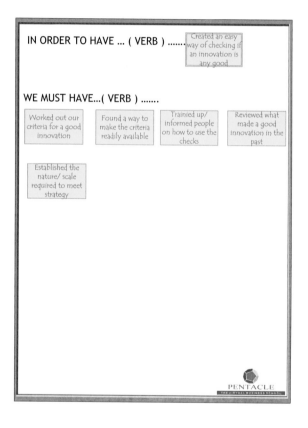

Which sticky to start with? Well it depends. A time line is normal but if you need to show progress or build credibility start on something easy. If you need to get attention from a stakeholder choose something they have to participate in.

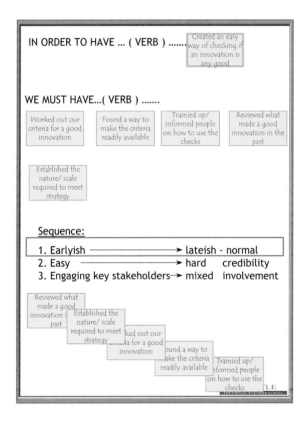

As we have repeated the process, tasks – things
we clearly know how to do – start to fall out. If
they don't, just repeat the process and break the
statement down further.

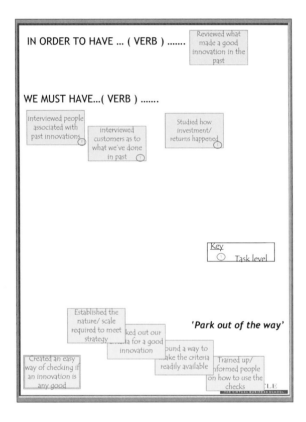

The clear, non-Foggy tasks can be given as accountabilities to the appropriate stakeholder.

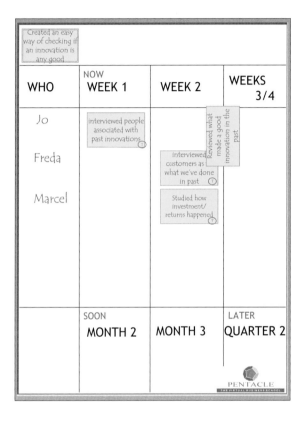

So now we have an estimate of how long the sub-project is going to take. Of course we'll review this in line with our 'drumbeat'.

WHO	NOW WEEK 1	WEEK 2	WEEKS 3/4
Jo	Interviewed people associated with past innovations ⓣ		Reviewed what made a good innovation in the past
Freda		interviewed customers as what we've done in past ⓣ	
Marcel		Studied how investment/returns happened ⓣ	
Me	Established the nature/ scale required to meet strategy		
Team			Worked out our criteria for a good innovation

	SOON MONTH 2	MONTH 3	LATER QUARTER 2
Team	Found a way to make the criteria readily available	Trained up/ informed people on how to use the checks	

Created an easy way of checking if an innovation is any good

PENTACLE
THE VIRTUAL BUSINESS SCHOOL

Finally, we can estimate the actual amount of work each task or sticky is likely to require.

From that we can estimate the level of resource required.

Your sticky step plan will answer the questions *'What to do? When to do it?, Who is accountable for getting it done?'* and will also have a stab at *'How to estimate the costs?'*

When I use this technique I usually do a dry run on my own to figure out who to invite to the main event and then I repeat it with the actual stakeholders. It works a treat!

So there we have it, a three-month-long sub-project, involving 4 people costing 29 person days. All you now have to do is finish off the Sticky Step^{TM} plan to work out how long the whole thing is going to take and how much resource it's going to consume. With that and with your gap analysis explaining what happens IF FIXED/IF NOT FIXED, I can see a business case coming on strongly.

Now remind me, why were you losing sleep?

Is your Project Organisation a Tangled Web?

So your sponsor, well you call him that, didn't
turn up for the steering group meeting it took
you a month to organise and which you're just
leaving. Perhaps it's just as well. That outburst
from the marketing manager, about the level of
disruption the project was causing to his part
of the business, was a bit embarrassing. And it
was also a bit embarrassing to have to explain,
as you went through the risk register update,
that it was almost certain that the platform
out-source supplier will not have the back-up
infrastructure in place in time for the hand-over.
No, embarrassing is the wrong word. All the
steering committee members used this as a cue to
kick you sharply in the ribs. Now as you sit down
at your desk and start on your e-mails, the first,
from the finance department, makes you emit an
audible groan. 'Oh no. Not another re-cut of the
budget and projected spends.' This is going to take
up half your afternoon. The phone rings. One of
your team members. A detailed question, to which
you do not know the answer. You suggest that they
talk directly to another team member. As soon as
you put the phone down it rings again. It's from
one of the unions representing some of your front-
line staff. He wants to know the details of your
planned roll out and to find out if there will be

any job losses as a result. He sounds very annoyed that he hadn't been informed before. Maybe you should have invited him to the steering committee meeting, but that wouldn't have been the right place to discuss his issues. Next e-mail. You've been asked to make yet another presentation to the Executive on the progress and risks your project poses to the organisation. You curse Turnbull and his report silently under your breath. Now you've got to stand up for yourself in front of the executive. You know that sponsor of yours won't add any value. It's at times like this that you think maybe having a decent sponsor wouldn't be so bad.

Did you recognise any of this? I hope not, but I suspect so. Organising a project is a good source of extra work and worry for the project leader. But organising a project isn't just about planning the tasks. The problem is that people don't always do what they are supposed to do when they are supposed to do it. The other skill is coordinating the contributions of all your stakeholders to arrive at the right quality, at the right level, without too much emotional upheaval to achieve a result they all view as success. I love that sentence, it makes it sound so easy.

The first problem is that most of us work in hierarchical organisations. Project implementation tends to ignore the niceties and fine intricacies of the power-political boundaries of the hierarchy, and simply drags a wide range of people into the melting pot. You have to reorganise and coordinate people who report to you, some who don't, many who are more powerful or senior to you, and many who have never even heard of you. Where do you start?

1. CREATING A STAKEHOLDER LIST IS ABSOLUTELY ESSENTIAL

The pre-requisite to organising others around you is to figure out who you need to organise for the project. For this, creating a stakeholder list of people **affected by it, needed to contribute to it, or needed on-side to allow it to progress,** is absolutely essential.

But simply knowing who your stakeholders are does not mean that you have coordinated and organised them. There are two further stages. You need to figure out how they fit into your 'project organisation'. As I said, most businesses organise their day to day work in a hierarchy of functions or departments. This approach is not very useful for a project which usually crosses those boundaries. You need your own organisation. A Project Organisation with clear roles and accountabilities.

2. FIGURE OUT THE ROLE EACH STAKEHOLDER IS TO PLAY IN YOUR ORGANISATION

If you've made a stakeholder list you have a good idea of what you think each person is bringing to the success of the project. So, great, you know their roles. But do they? Do they really know what they are supposed to be contributing, what is expected from them and what they are accountable for?

3. MAKE SURE THAT EVERYONE IN YOUR PROJECT ORGANISATION UNDERSTANDS THEIR ROLE AND CONTRIBUTION AND THE CROSS DEPENDENCIES THEY HAVE WITH OTHER STAKEHOLDERS

You also need to be sure that you keep them tightly bound and managed throughout the project. No risks, no ticking time bombs, no political surprises.

I usually propose a 'web' to catch and hold all the stakeholders in. Once caught you will be able to efficiently organise them. The Project Web acts as a checklist, and also can be used as a working tool simply by writing people's names on the framework.

The web has six sticky areas:

1. The project customers, project clients and key contacts

> *'That outburst from the marketing manager about the level of disruption the project was causing to his part of the business was a bit embarrassing.'*

Overall role: to make sure that the project benefit is achieved by continually checking both the hard and soft success criteria, and ensuring that the organisation is ready and capable to accept the benefit.

The Project OrganoWeb

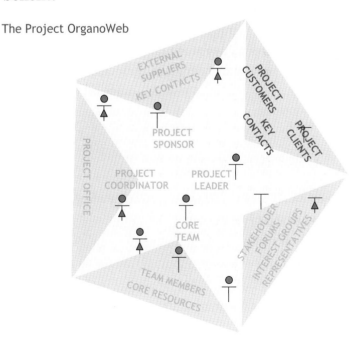

This involves the people who have to live with the outcomes of the project and/or are clearly identified with its implementation. (I detest the use of the expressions 'The users' – drug takers perhaps? 'The Business' – implies that the project team are external suppliers perhaps trying to rip-off their colleagues?)

- *Project customers* are the consumers of the benefits of the project.

- *Project clients* are often paying for the project implementation. Sometimes (and I recommend this) a second and often primary sponsor is from this group.

- *Key contacts* have a goal of supporting the project implementation and act as a conduit and focal point for the needs of this group. An excellent working relationship with the key contacts is usually needed if you are to succeed.

2. Stakeholder forums, interest groups, representatives

'He sounds very annoyed that he hadn't been informed before. Maybe you should have invited him to the steering committee meeting, but that

wouldn't have been the right place to discuss his issues.'

Overall role: to provide a discussion space to resolve common issues shared by different groups of stakeholders. The role of the participants is to explore the downstream implications of the project, put their point of view whilst listening to other points of views and ensuring that the broadest agreement is reached.

This is about bringing together groups of stakeholders who might have different views on the project, to help them thrash out the issues together amongst themselves. Many projects have a steering group or committee as a forum.

The Project OrganoWeb

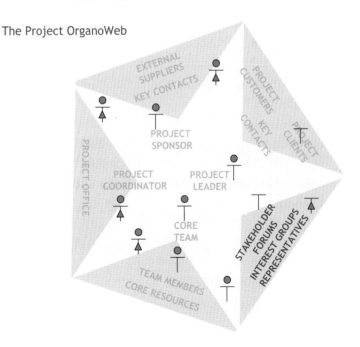

The problem comes when the project leader fails to tell them clearly their role and the purpose of the forum. In some projects, these forums might bring together external constituencies of stakeholders like unions or local residents. In several organisations trying to manage corporate risk and make it transparent to their shareholders, it is common for an executive meeting to act as one of the forums that fall into the project leader's OrganoWeb.

3. External suppliers, key contacts

'And it was also a bit embarrassing to have to explain, as you went through the risk register update, that it was almost certain that the platform out-source supplier will not have the back-up infrastructure in place in time for the hand-over.'

Overall role: to provide timely, quality, cost-effective inputs and outcomes that the organisation itself does not have the capability to deliver.

4. Project office

'... the first, from the finance department makes you emit an audible groan. Not another re-cut of the budget and projected spends. This is going to take up half your afternoon.'

Overall role: to provide common project management processes and language across the organisation. To provide tools, training and support for integration with the rest of the organisation, such as financial or project planning, and providing appropriate work environments e.g. test vs. development.

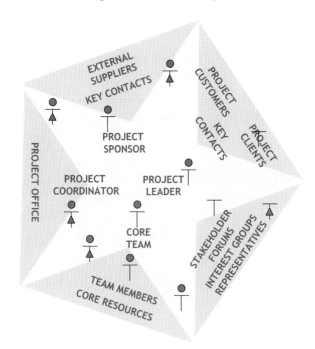

5. Core resources/wider team

'... one of your team members. A detailed question which you know you can't answer. You suggest that they talk directly to another team member. As soon as you put the phone down it rings again.'

The role of this group is to help carry the heavy load. To provide specialist contributions and to act as ambassadors across the organisation.

6. The project delivery team

The project delivery team is the backbone, the heart and the brain of the change operation. To fully understand the project delivery team, you need to look at the individual roles in this sub-section, breaking them into specific and separate roles: you – the leader, the sponsor, the core team and the project coordinator. Sometimes the leader and coordinator roles are combined.

The sponsor role is the rarest to find being carried well. I guess for many senior executives they aren't even sure why a project needs sponsoring. My advice is, if your project doesn't have a sponsor, find one. The sponsor is usually a person who:

- invented the idea and really wants to do it

- controls the money

- wants the end product or will end up living with it

- can provide effective high level representation, and smooth out the political battles before you get to them

- 'owns' the resources

- acts as an effective sounding board/mentor

- is the manager or director of the programme the project belongs to.

This prevents the nightmare ...

'So your sponsor, well you call him that, didn't turn up for the steering group meeting ...'

A core team is the group of people you select to be intimately involved in the project. You may have discovered by now that it is pretty difficult to forge more than eight people into a team. **My rule of thumb is to keep the core team to about five** – it's easier to get meetings arranged with the smaller number, and when you discuss issues there is enough 'air-time' for everyone. If you need a bigger team, you can get each of your core team to manage a team around them, so even a team of 100 is only three people deep (you lead 5 who lead 5 who lead 5). I also find that it is easier to be clear on accountabilities.

To select the best people for your core team, select a person who:

- influences outcome significantly towards success or failure

- is integrated with other stakeholders and others 'interdepend' on them for success

- possesses appropriate skills, knowledge and behaviour to match the type of project you are running

- possesses the appropriate role or position in the organisation for some of the key activities which need to be carried out

- has time/resources to stay throughout, and be committed and carry out lots of work

- believes in the project

- is dedicated, enthusiastic and a good ambassador for the project

- performs core tasks which are absolutely necessary day-to-day to get the job done.

The project coordinator's role is to provide administrative and communications support for the delivery team and to interface with the project office.

A real example I'm involved in at the moment looks like this:

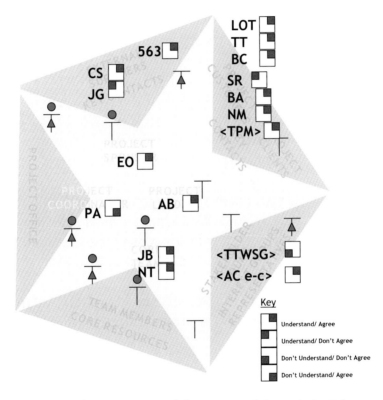

The project is an invisible, internal 'movie' with all the classic risks that poses, of getting carried away by the technology, rather than focusing on the project customer's benefits. Names and initials have been changed to protect the guilty, I mean innocent.

So far, we've made sure all the stakeholders are aware of their roles, especially the project customers BA, BC, LOT, TT and NM. As sponsor, I've done this by personally visiting each one to start the emotional engagement process, and to get them to agree to be involved in the development and prototyping.

Meanwhile, our Project Leader AB has done all the groundwork on the supplier interface, to de-risk that as much as possible and ensure technical success.

As you can see, there is still some work to be done on the forum called TTWSG, so I shall need to schedule a number of meetings with them.

And JG still needs to be listened to, and brought on side. Finally, we have to hope that the core team can cope with the workload because there aren't any other core resources.

Our project manager still needs to share the full diagram with all the stakeholders, so that they can be aware of who the other stakeholders are.

Use the Project Web as a thinking and working framework. Tangle your stakeholders up in it and keep them organised.

The Project Leader's Decision Making Process

You're waiting for your VP to approve the additional budget spend you need. You've been wondering what can be so difficult. True there are six other projects in the programme – but yours is the lead enabler, the linchpin. Now you've just heard that you're going to have to present to the Exec. And now one of your team has approached you to ask whether they should hold a user meeting to agree the prototype before it's completely finished. You're not sure, your users are an awkward bunch. You never know if it's better to involve them or keep them in the dark. It's hard to know.

So what is this thing, a decision? A decision is something that happens to select a route at a crossroads – a choice of ways forward, at the end of a phase of the journey, we are going to stop doing, start doing. The reason they are worrying is because usually decisions are hard to reverse – if you've spent your budget it's gone! And decisions have implications.

The main difference between project decision making and 'normal' decision making is that on projects, the decisions you make come back to haunt you in the future, as the project carries on. For example, in a line job – a customer isn't happy? Give them a refund – Problem solved. In a project

– a stakeholder isn't happy? Give them a better spec. Problem solved. But now your budget will be overspent or you will have additional time pressure so your team are going to have to work harder and morale is going to dip, and the change in spec will trigger a change management process with a sign-off by your sponsor who may not agree to the change in spec a week later – so you'll have to go back to the unhappy stakeholder and break the news that you can't give them what you promised. In projects remember the first law of change, **One Change Leads to Another**.

The first thing to be clear on is whose decision it is. I call this big and little decisions. **If it's yours** to make I call it a **decision**. **If it is for others** to influence or make I call it a **Decision**.

I've discovered, from years of running project management computer simulations, that you can substantially increase the performance of a team in a short period by making sure that they have a common decision-making process. A good process can make up for a lack of project management experience in the team. The strange thing is that a good process works just as well in real life as it does in front of a computer. The five-step process I teach is called the project manager's decision-making process. For tackling decisions it is:

1 What is the BIG **Issue?**

2 Who are the **Stakeholders** involved?

3 What do I, as the leader, **Want** to happen?

4 What are my **Options**? (always include the 'do nothing' option)

5 If I do this option ... what do I expect to happen **Next**?

I have a terrible mnemonic for this which is ISWON.

Issue**S**takeholders**W**ant**O**ptions**N**ext?

(For some groups that I teach BISIMODN – pronounced busy moden – seems to work better – **B**ig**I**ssue**S**takeholders**I**nvolved**M**y**O**ptions**D**o**N**ext).

The BIG Issue is my shortcut way of saying, 'what's actually going on?' For example, a team member not achieving their deliverable may appear to be a performance issue. But if you step back and think about all the other things connected with the team member you may realise that the big issue is inclusion – the team member doesn't really feel included in the team and has no problem in letting everyone down.

Once you have been through the process you need to check that you are maintaining stakeholder engagement. Remember the second law of change,

People create change – People constrain change. Let them help you invent the decision and they'll get hooked on making it happen – surprise them with your decision and they'll fight you all the way. So it's essential to check where they stand and make sure you keep them engaged. I use a simple 2 × 3 matrix. List all the stakeholders you need to agree and all the stakeholders you'll need to do the work and then decide whether you need to involve them in the actual decision making process or whether it will just be enough to consult or inform them.

STAKEHOLDER ENGAGEMENT MAP

The process is the same if it is a Decision. The main difference is that you have to make sure

People you need

	to agree	to do work
to involve		
People you need to consult		
to inform (in advance)		

someone else goes through the project manager's decision process. To make this happen you will have to have some additional information.

- **Whose** Decision is it?

- **What** is the Decision to be made? – As clearly and concisely as possible.

- **Why** does it need to be made? – Use the impact/worst or best case analysis to help.

- **How long** is it valid for?

	Forum	
	multiple 1:1	group meeting
discussion/ consensus	Good emotional engagement Implications fully understood	Good emotional engagement Implications on each other understood
Method voting	May be affected by non-related agendas	No emotional engagement Often will not result in action People who voted against may not accept cabinet decision
authority - announce	No engagement Will see compliance behaviours	No engagement Opposition have a chance to find out who their allies might be Compliance behaviours

The final wrinkle is to make sure that you've chosen the right method for making the decision. Different methods will lead to different behaviours from stakeholders.

Perhaps this is why your VP was taking so long over making the budget decision and why it's best for you to make your presentation to the Exec. And perhaps you should involve those awkward users – not letting them see the prototype might mean that what happens next ... is that they become completely obstructive!

LEARNING AND REVIEW

Getting effective review to happen is almost
impossible. If the project is going well why
bother reviewing? If it's going badly there
is obviously no time to review. And if it's
going really terribly, a real disaster, then
no one wants to review in case when we
review 'they find out the problem is me!'

Always plan your reviews exactly as you
would plan your tasks and activities.

Learning means doing something different.
Many project managers can manage
P-D-R, Plan-Do Review. Good, but pointless.
I recommend P-D-R-L-AD Plan-Do
Review-Learn-Act Differently.

I have one piece for you here.
projectcommunication@netspeed is a
distillation of many of the tools, techniques
and tips I have found useful. Live and
unlearn!

eo

project.communication
@netspeed

It's been one of those days. It's six o'clock and you still haven't left the office. You still have 12 more e-mails to go. Your whole day has been a blur and you haven't even made any progress on your 'To Do' list. It all began at half past eight this morning when you opened your first e-mail of the day from your sponsor, demanding an explanation of why specific changes he's asked for in the final design hadn't been incorporated. You're straight on the phone to chase this up. You listen as the phone rings and rings. After about thirty rings you become increasingly impatient – you had at least expected it to divert to voice mail – but nothing! Another five rings and you hang up in disgust. You have five more minutes to respond to a few more e-mails – all except one – bad news – all bad news you could have predicted if you'd thought enough about it in advance – you half wish you hadn't opened them. The only one which isn't bad news, could be bad news, but it is long and written in so much detail and has seven pages of attached history, so you aren't really sure what the message was. Anyway, you've filed it. If it was important it will come back again. You race down the corridor to the first of your three meetings. The meetings roll one into another, lots of talk and when all's said and done, a lot more's been said than done. And nothing's been done since the previous meeting anyway. You spend the rest of the morning playing phone tag with your team member – the one who you had specifically asked to incorporate the changes your sponsor is upset about. The lunch time audio conference with the US is as boring and non-involving as always, and as always your VP drones on in a steady monotone without breathing, definitely not allowing any response or questions. As always, the issues he is talking about are a month overdue and everyone has already found workarounds. As always, it overruns and blows your schedule of reporting and update meetings for the afternoon and that is why at six pm you are still finishing off the day's e-mails.

There is definitely something wrong. Cyberspace was to be our saviour – communication at the speed of light was supposed to improve our lives. Meetings were supposed to improve communication and allow us to work more effectively with others. Global working was supposed to allow us to share learning so that we wouldn't spend our lives reinventing the wheel. Somehow, instead of speeding up our projects, all the technological advances seem to do is to make more complex work happen slower with more misunderstanding.

Again, the New World[5] of enterprise has pulled another fast one on us – by appearing to give us choice and opportunities we haven't noticed that, as usual, it has changed the rules of success in five subtle but powerful ways.

1. IT IS IMPORTANT TO RECOGNISE THAT DATA IS NOT INFORMATION

Have you ever deleted an e-mail you were sent because it was useless to you? A situation. My first real job was with Shell. I arrived at work on the first day to find that there was a stack of mail and letters waiting for me. The correspondence wasn't addressed to me but to FMB1/4. You see, we had job numbers so you could send messages to the job, knowing that the current incumbent would find the message as useful as the previous incumbent – I suspect this idea no longer works in your organisation.

I had fun a few years ago. I was invited to talk at a major conference for information professionals. I was the keynote speaker, and walked on stage and announced that 'I shouldn't really be here talking to Information Professionals, because I myself don't know what information is!' There was a silence. No response. And then I asked, 'Could

---

[5] From *New Rules for the New World*, Eddie Obeng, Capstone.

you help me? What is information?' Silence. 'OK.
If I said 42, would that be information?' Silence.
'Come on, you're professionals, surely you know
the answer – Put your hand up if you think this
is information.' Some hands went up. I said,
'What's missing?' Someone shouted 'We need
more.' I said, '42 years. Is that enough?' 'Give us
context!' a voice cried. '42 years old. How about
that?' I'd proved my point. Although they were
supposed to be information professionals, they
themselves, like most people, had little idea of
what information actually is. Next I said, 'What's
missing?' Someone shouted, 'The question!' I
reply, 'Precisely – If you had asked, "How old
are you Eddie?" and I had replied, '42 years old',
we would have **question plus data leading to an
answer – information.**' Everyone laughed. I said,
'The only problem is that I'm not 42 years old. So

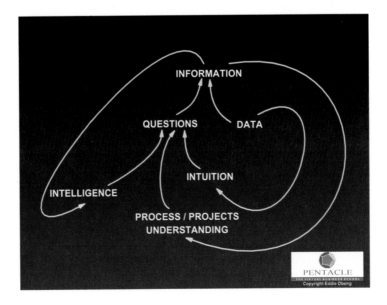

although it would have been wrong information, it would have been information all the same.' Again, laughter.

Whenever you communicate you must ask yourself, **'What question does this answer for the person I'm communicating with?'**

Also, make sure that your answer isn't too detailed. For a shorthand, you can think of **three levels** of detail – passing your sponsor in the corridor, he enquires about progress. You reply with the big picture (Level 1). You meet a colleague or project customer.[6] They enquire about progress. You list the issues but not much more (Level 2). This time it's a team member – you launch into the full details (Level 3). Imagine what would happen if you got the level wrong!

So now you can tell others about how to communicate at the right level, so that you will never again need *to spend your time reading and filing e-mails which are long and written in so much detail and have seven pages of attached history so you aren't really sure what the message is.*

---

[6] I dislike the expressions 'user', 'the business', etc. I use the expression 'project customer'.

2. *YOUR ORGANISATION DESIGN IS PROBABLY WRONG*

A fact. The speed of information is getting faster by about a factor of ten every 3 years (this is faster than computers, which only double their speed every 18 months). In most organisations, the information travels around the organisation at about 100 Mb/s and comes into the organisation at about 10 Mb/s.

Another fact. There is a maximum speed at which information can be transferred to a group of senior executives (about 1 Mb/s for 25).

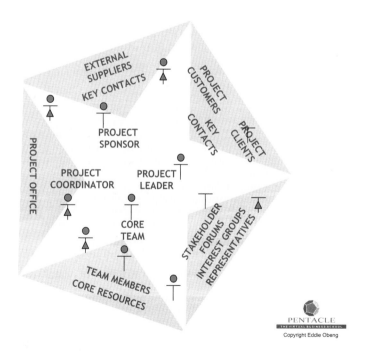

A resulting fact. In the New World, if your business is organised as a command and control hierarchy, your senior executives will be your corporate bottleneck.

Another resulting fact. If your project relies on a steering group as its main decision and influence stakeholder group, progress will be slow with significant rework.

You need to design your own personal organisation structure. This structure should be based around all the stakeholders of your project. Identify **who will be affected by the project** (especially those who will have to change their behaviour as a result of the project), **those you need to take along** (or else they will slow or block progress), and **those you need as resources**. Put the names of these people on the diagram below.

Which stakeholders are critical to success?			
	Name	Issue	Solution
As resources			
To take along			
To ensure that the benefit is reaped			

Stakeholder	Relationship	Communication When (before decision?)	Frequency	How (touch/cyberspace)

Once you have worked out who these people are, you need to **create a communication plan**. The plan should tell you when to communicate with them (e.g. before or after decisions), how frequently, the medium and method, and ensure that they are aware of their role in the communication.

So now you understand why *you will end up spending more and more of your time listening, as your VP drones on in a steady monotone talking about issues that are about a month overdue.*

3. THE NEW WORLD DOESN'T GIVE YOU A SECOND CHANCE IN COMMUNICATION - IT SIMPLY MOVES ON

It is best to get your communication across the first time before any actions are taken.

There is a question that is forbidden to anyone even vaguely interested in becoming a competent project or change manager. Do you know what this question is? Probably not. I'm sure that as a New World project leader, you've never, ever asked the forbidden question. The forbidden question is, 'Do you understand?' Useless! Pointless and Wasteful. You might as well walk up to a complete stranger and say, 'Snurgisterloop?'

Why is it so useless? Imagine you say to someone 'Do you understand?' – what answer are you almost inevitably bound to get? If they understand, they will reply, 'Yes'. If they don't understand, but they don't know that they don't understand, they will still say, 'Yes'. If they don't understand, but are too embarrassed to say so, they will still say 'Yes!' In some cultures, the only acceptable answer anyway is 'Yes'. You see why this question is as effective as asking 'Snurgisterloop?'

So what question should you ask? No, don't ask them to repeat what you just said, or ask, 'What did I just say?' – Parrots are good at imitation but not good at comprehension – another 'Snurgisterloop?' No, don't ask them how they feel about it, or if it's OK. – 'Snurgisterloop?'

So what question should you ask? One of a select group. Ask instead, '**What are the implications for you?** What are you going to do as a result of what I've just said? How will this affect you next?' This type of question forces them to learn. They have to try to remember **what** you said, **reflect** on what it means for them, try to work out the **implications** or effects of your statements, and then work out and **plan** the actions they need to take as a result – Learning. *Now you will never again have to open an e-mail from your sponsor demanding why specific changes he's asked for in the final design hadn't been incorporated, or playing phone tag*

*with your team members you had specifically
asked to incorporate the changes.*

**Remember most project mistakes come from
the simple fact that the project leader assumes
a situation or implications for a stakeholder and
doesn't bother to check this.**

4. THE NEW WORLD HAS CREATED STRICT BUT SECRET RULES ON HOW AND WHEN TO USE TOUCHSPACE[7] AND CYBERSPACE

Two scenarios.

(a) Have you ever started an argument by e-mail
and then discovered that the only way to
resolve it was to sit down face to face?

(b) Have you ever been ensnared in an e-mail web
where a dozen or so people are e-mailing each
other, copying each other in on some mails
and not on others, weaving in the odd corridor
meeting and then eventually, someone
sensible phones round saying, after all that
time invested in carefully worded e-mails,
'We need to have a meeting to discuss this.'

---

[7] My word from *New Rules for the New World* to describe
the non-electronic world human beings, tables and plants
inhabit. The world where you can physically contact and
touch things.

The reason is that e-mail doesn't work in all situations. You see, communication has to deal with **a range of emotional situations** and a range of communication from the **simple to the complex** – the sort of issue which requires a large number of people to discuss and interact, before full comprehension and agreement is reached. Touchspace and cyberspace inhabit different regions of this grid.

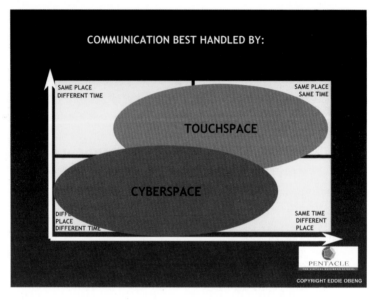

And more importantly, the range of tools we have operate effectively only in specific areas of the grid.

So think about the tool you are about to use before you choose it. Always adapt it, *don't play phone tag – leave a message suggesting a time for a phone meeting – or e-mail to agree a time.* Audio conferences need rules, (you can interrupt by saying, 'excuse me', you must say your name before you make your point, etc.), a strong coordinator, a break for comments from the participants every 5–7 minutes, no more, *not allowing any response or questions*, a summary of points covered and agreed actions at least every 15–20 minutes, and should last no longer than 40 minutes (remember two-thirds of people take on information through visual images and actual physical cues).

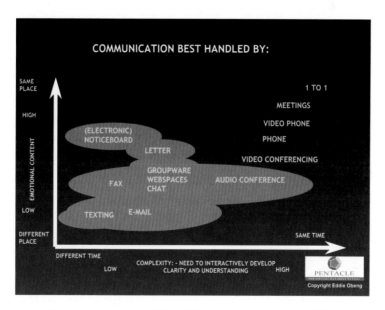

Another important idea I have championed is the use of **'hybrid tools™'**. For example, at Pentacle The Virtual Business School we are more likely to use a combination of an audio conference and a webspace than a video conference. We find that such a hybrid tool is more effective. We

routinely use meetings/groupware or meetings/
e-mail where the discussion and actions of the
meeting and the minutes are typed up (shown
on the projector so that everyone can see what's
going down) during the meeting, directly into a
group space or onto e-mails which arrive at the
participants' desks before they leave the meeting!

5. IN THE NEW WORLD, THE PAST ISN'T WHAT IT USED TO BE

In the Old World, in most organisations, yesterday
was very similar to today and today to tomorrow.
So an obsession with review was not only an
intelligent thing, it was also effective. If you
reported on what had happened, this provided good
cues on what might happen next and what should
be done!

In most organisations, reporting is about **passive**
events in the **past**. 'The spend was $30,000', etc.
It's like a **history lesson** of dates, events and
kings. But then the question which is always
asked is, 'Why $30,000?' at which point an **active**
explanation is provided – a **fairy tale!** 'Ah well,
it was because …'. Interesting, but pointless. The
money has already been spent. And if tomorrow is
going to be different from today, not even a good
clue.

A New World project manager focuses instead on what might happen next and how it might come about!

The split in time between **review/preview**™ should be more like 20/80 rather than as it is in most projects of 90/10.

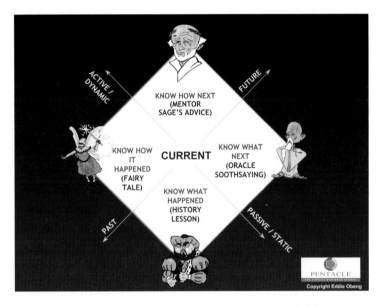

So now you can avoid *bad news you could have predicted if you'd thought enough about it in advance.*

Understanding the five rules of success should help you to achieve project.communication@netspeed but the biggest tip I have for you is: never open your e-mail first thing in the morning. Give yourself at least half an hour of planning and organising time before you become a 'reactive overactive'.

THE VISION THING ...

I delivered perfect.projects@netspeed
as a paper in a ra-ra fashion to the
International Project Management
Conference in Paris in September 2001.

I enjoyed myself thoroughly, got a bit
too excited and talked really fast.

I got through this rather long piece in
about half an hour! It's a good grounding
in my work. Hope you enjoy it and I hope
you find the tortoise!

eo

perfect.projects@netspeed

THE NEW WORLD OF BUSINESS

The last decade has taken us on a whirlwind journey. Social and technological change have provided opportunities for enterprise which have led to the explosion of communication, travel, trade and infrastructure changes such as the Internet. **Each opportunity exploited simply creates another**. For example, the availability of a graphical user interface allowed the development of browsers, which in turn allowed the development of websites requiring better browsers with faster access than a modem, to digital connections and so on, almost exponentially. And even when the market slows, you must adapt, so change accelerates and your workload and pressures go up! Large drops in share prices lead to opportunities for deals, acquisition and merger and synergies requiring retraining, re-organisation and so on, almost exponentially.

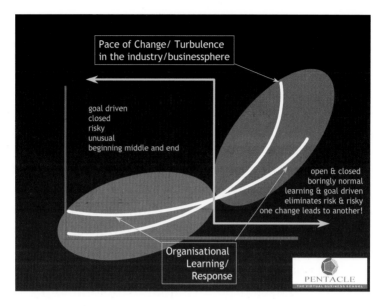

THE NEW WORLD IS THE ENVIRONMENT
YOU FIND YOURSELF IN WHEN THE PACE
OF CHANGE/COMPLEXITY IN THE WORLD
OUTSIDE YOUR ORGANSIATION OUTSTRIPS
YOUR ORGANISATION'S ABILITY TO LEARN
AND ADAPT.

Change is the cause and the effect of itself.

Unfortunately, organisations, including yours, are caught up in this buffeting. Buffeted by tides and changes greater than themselves. Most organisations are 'creatures of habit', preferring the industry sectors they understand to the business-sphere they don't. Preferring internally driven programmes to those inspired from outside the organisation, say by customers. For many organisations their concession to their customers in a wired world is a website, developed by an out-source supplier, which is simply an animated version of a corporate brochure or annual report. This leaves a real opportunity and advantage for any competitor who takes the time to carry out real change, big change, effectively and successfully.

Now change feeds on change to the point where, for most organisations, the pace of change in their business-sphere has outstripped their ability to learn and change. This is the New World.

BIG CHANGE TAMED

In the New World the opportunities for change are almost endless. In the 1990s the focus of most enterprises was on change, but simultaneous change – the type found in operations, processes and procedures. Improving, redesigning and re-engineering them ran a close second to realigning functional reporting lines as a way of getting better, of getting change to happen.

After a long but unsuccessful innings enterprises began to realise that to alter anything at all in the organisation, from its structure to its supply chain to its market access, required that they learnt how to tame change, how to deliver BIG change, how to deliver sequential, discontinuous change. Either that or start with a headcount reduction and let luck and nature take its course.

Programmes and projects have taken over from processes and procedures.

They discovered the need to deliver very big change by breaking it into smaller chunks.[8] They have begun to understand that, in the New World with significant change, it becomes effective to ensure that the projects (chunks of change) are aligned closely into programmes (big flocks of chunks, which, like birds, fly in the same direction close to each other) in order to have effective implementation. They have discovered the essential need in the New World to manage projects and programmes of change.

This is the decade of the project and programme manager.

---

[8] A chunk is a word for piece, like you'd break off a loaf of bread by hand or off a cold bar of chocolate.

PREDICTABLE CHANGE

Now we have begun to understand that projects
go wrong following common patterns. My now
famous and widely published bubble diagram
summarises the typical ways in which projects go
wrong and why.

We've begun to understand how to interface a
project or programme and its organisation with
the rest of the enterprise. Now we have begun
to understand what tools to use, and when, the
importance of stakeholders, the critical difference
between open and closed change. We've begun
to understand how, in the New World, projects
exist against a backdrop of uncertainty. Often
we cannot completely pre-plan everything
but have to evolve the plan during the project,
whilst at the same time risk and loss of focus
become real threats. This creates for us a range
of intended 'chunks of change' – projects, from
'Foggy' (something must be done but what and
how?) through **Quests** (the goal is known but
not the method) and **Movies** (the technology or
method is decided but the deliverables have to be
negotiated) to the traditional and closed **'Painting-
by-numbers'** projects (goals and methods known).

*If you understand what type of change
you're dealing with the issues are about 95%
predictable.*

We have begun to understand why a significant
proportion of joint ventures end acrimoniously. In
several countries the legal system is being revised
to encourage completion of projects, to deliver
benefits rather than legal wrangles, which result
in non-completion. The belief is that some benefits
are better than none.

As New World project and programme change
management becomes more precise, *the focus
needs to shift from the **delivery** of the project to
ensuring that a real **benefit** is achieved.*

THE TYPE OF PROJECT YOU END UP WITH
DEPENDS ON HOW FAST YOUR LEARNING
IS (HAS BEEN) COMPARED TO THE PACE OF
CHANGE IN THE WORLD

GLOBAL CHANGE

In the next decade our ambitiousness on both project and programme delivery will continue to increase. As 'global' becomes a standard scale even for medium sized organisations, programmes and projects will routinely have to cope with rapidly building teams made up of multiple national cultures. *A good ability to lead and develop virtual team working will be essential.* And the ability to create 3 × 8 hr teams (where three implementation teams pass the baton from one team to the other around the globe on 8hr shifts per day from London to New York to Tokyo) and many other new forms of work will be required.

Leading across cultures and virtual teams requires a full 'utility belt' of tools and the ability to create an overriding supportive environment.

Of these, the most challenging will probably be that of quickly creating a common project/ programme culture across different national cultures.

WEB-ENABLED CHANGE

The ever-pervasive web of the Internet will provide the unique infrastructure for supporting projects. It will provide training and development for you, the project leaders and programme managers. It will provide the tools that you will use for knowledge management, reporting and communication. It will provide the link between you and the stakeholder benefits that the programme or project is to achieve.

The web is the tortoise upon whose back we create our New World of programmes and projects

It will provide just-in-time advice lines and expert guidance and opportunities for collaboration.

CHANGE AS THE ORGANISATIONAL STRUCTURE

In the coming decade projects and programmes will further eat into the Old World hierarchical, command and control, functional structure of organisations as the relative amount of repetitive, operations/process based activity declines in favour of the upgradable, one-off project/ programme activity. It will make less and less sense to think of a career in linear hierarchical terms.

If change is the norm, the organisation structure and environment ought to reflect it.

To think of a function such as marketing being anything other than just a long string of programmes will seem old fashioned.

DELIVERING CHANGE IN A NEW WORLD

The New World encourages the faster, more-effective delivery of successful projects at an increasing pace. The key factors of **speed**, **perspective** and **discipline** become essential to the success of programmes and projects. However, to achieve speed it is essential to understand the place and role of stakeholders in order to achieve **emotional engagement** and, as a result, to reduce resistance to change. To achieve perspective, it is important for the project always to be viewed from the big picture of the enterprise as well as the immediate objectives.

Speed, perspective and discipline beat everything else.

The development of project leaders, the development and fulfilment of team members' aspirations, and the guidance and support of the programme managers all contribute to the disciplined delivery of benefit.

HARVESTING THE BENEFITS OF CHANGE

I also believe that our ability to understand and implement big change using projects and programmes will make us more selective of the challenges we take on. The focus on benefits will mean the death of functional and departmental projects. All projects will be business projects.

Change and improvement are not the same thing. With improvement there is benefit. It's because of the benefit that we bother to change.

Enabling and infrastructure projects will transform themselves to be intricately linked with the benefits that they underpin. They will no longer stand alone.

SKILLS FOR CREATING A NEW WORLD

When I grow up I want to be ... a project leader?

A statement never or rarely heard from a 5 year old, and yet the New World makes the roles of a project leader and programme manager more exciting and challenging than they have ever been.

The future is bright based on what we have learnt in the past, the basics of project success. To your advantage, project leadership and programme management will continue to be the most transferable and sought-after management skills.

JIGSAW

Fitting the Pieces Together in the New World Project Management Approach

I put this six-page PMA together one week when I got fed up with a 100-page project management approach I was working on for a client. It contains all the really crucial, key questions and tools needed to deliver your Perfect Project. You can cut it out of the book or you can download it from PentacleTheVBS.com/PerfectProjects.htm or from within the AllChange club (remember the password on page 3). The only copyright stipulation is that it must always be on a yellow background. So if you wish to print it out you'll need to find some yellow paper.

eo

The New World Approach to Managing Change & Projects

JIGSAW

AllChange.com

Change with the right Purpose, matched to the right Project Type, derisked and kept on track through effective Learning and Review, set up with good Planning and Coordination plus effective Stakeholder Management, shared amongst the team, multiplied by (your) effective Leadership, equals Success

Purpose,
Change/
Project Type

Learning
& review

Planning and
co-ordination

Stakeholder
Management

Leadership &
Team management

$$\left(\frac{(P,C/PT*L\&R) +P\&C +SHM}{T} \right) * L = Success$$

Continuously check:

1. Work out why the project is being done.
Identify key stakeholders (especially the sponsor)
Identify change/ project type.
Assess risk and set up risk management process

2. Select the best method
work out what each stage means for your change/ project and add in extra actions depending on stakeholders visibility and driver/deliverer

3. Decide on hard and soft success criteria
Establish what is in and what is out
Create a stakeholder management strategy

4. Keep building your team
Follow the project type typical stages selecting tools from the toolbox (or working with cyberFranck)

5. Close out (and hand over to process) to ensure that after the effort the benefits are gained

Project Name

Sponsor

Date of request

Work out why the project is being done. Identify key stakeholders (especially the sponsor) Identify change / project type. Assess risk and set up risk management process

1

Why is the Project needed?
(A bubble diagram or gap analysis will help explain)

ATTACH BUBBLES/GAPS

What key issues will it resolve?
(top of bubbles - implications of gap analysis)

What improvement will be achieved?
(check your money making machine questions)

How is it chunked to ensure that effort and benefits are achieved
(min effort for max benefit? Check V vs. w vs. L vs. A)

ATTACH BENIFLOW LINE

What type of project is it?

☐ Painting-by-numbers   ☐ Visible   ☐ Change

☐ Quest   ☐ Invisible   ☐ Commercial

☐ Fog   ☐ Turnkey

☐ Movie   ☐ Agency

☐ Joint venture

ATTACH OBENG PROJECT CUBE

Key stakeholders are:
(why are these people key stakeholders?)

What immediate or continuing actions will you be taking as a result of the project type? (see crystal ball gazing)

What are the severe risks to overall project success and how are they to be managed?

ATTACH RISK ANALYSIS

ATTACH GAZING INTO THE FUTURE

PINNACLE

Project Name [   ]　　**Project Type** [   ] [   ]

What method will you be using?

ATTACH METHOD

2　**What additional stages will you be adding to the method.**

S elect the best method work out what each stage means for your change/project and add in extra actions depending on stakeholders visibility and driver/deliverer

When are the key milestones (P b - n)

When are the time/money limits (Quest)

What is your drumbeat? (Fog)

When is the requirements specification signoff? (Movie)

What issues do you anticipate with which stakeholders?
(having completed your stakeholder map will help)

Name	Issue	Solution
Dracula		
Fence post Holder		
Punters		

ATTACH STAKEHOLDER MAP

Which stakeholders are critical to success?

	Name	Issue	Solution
As resources			
To take along			
To ensure that the benefit is reaped			

Which stakeholders/ stakeholder issues do you need help from your sponsor with?

Stakeholder	Relationship	Communication When (before decision?)	Frequency	How (touch/cyberspace)
. . . . .				

ATTACH STAKEHOLDER MAP

Direct, Barter, Sell, Lower and raise, Curveball, up and over/Trojan Horse

PENTACLE

Project Name

Hard Success Criteria

Plot the Project centre of gravity (Your view)

Plot the views of your key stakeholders

Timeliness

3

Decide on hard and soft success criteria
Create a TOR or scope or storyboard
Create a stakeholder management strategy

Money

Defined requirement

Money

Internal
External
Total Amount

Timeliness

Before/After
Date

Defined Requirements.

Metrics

ATTACH FINANCE PLAN/
BUSINESS PLAN/ REQUIREMENTS
SPECIFICATION

What actions/issues are to be taken to resolve the mismatch in hard criteria?

What actions need to be carried out to secure the money you can spend (budget)?

Soft Success Criteria

What are the key soft measures of success?

How will you monitor the soft criteria?

What ground rules will you set for your team/ stakeholders to increase the chances of success?

ATTACH HOPES & FEARS

Get TOR agreed/signed off

B ACKGROUND What is the background of this project. Who initiated it and why is it being done

O BJECTIVES What is it trying to achieve and how will it be measured

S COPE What is the scope of the project in terms of its boundaries. (What is in and what is not!

C ONSTRAINTS What is Timeliness/Cost/Specification/Quality Also Environment/Social/Legal/Commercial

A SSUMPTIONS What assumptions have been made in respect to this project.

R EPORTING What to report, when, to whom, and with what media

S CHEDULE Time schedule at the appropriate level to show Time, Who, Task, Deliverable, Dependencies

ATTACH TOR

Project Name

Project Type

PENTACLE

Keep building your team

Follow the project type typical stages selecting tools from the toolbox (or working with cyberFranck)

4

What method are you using to create your schedule? (elements of a schedule Who, What By When?)
- ☐ Sticky Steps
- ☐ Critical Path Analysis

ATTACH SCHEDULE

What method are you using to manage and communicate your schedule?

What People / Resources do you need and when?

What Review process will you be implementing?

ATTACH YOUR REFLECTION SCORE

What actions are you going to take to appropriately unbalance your team?

Customising your team (Unbalancing)
What behaviours predominate in your team?
Carer☐ Solver☐ Doer☐ Knower☐ Checker☐

What behaviours do you wish to see more of in your team?
Carer☐ Solver☐ Doer☐ Knower☐ Checker☐

Creating a team of interdependence (ICO)
What is your preferred Leadership Situation?

Checking your leadership behaviours:

What actions are you taking to improve inclusion?

What actions will you be taking to ensure you demonstrate effective behaviours?

ATTACH LEADERSHIP BEHAVIOUR AUDIT

What actions are you taking to overcome control barriers?

What are your high risk tasks?
(critical not done before)

Who are your high risk people?

ATTACH TASK RISK GRID

ATTACH PEOPLE RISK GRID

What actions are you planning to increase openness?

How will you manage changes introduced by stakeholders?

ATTACH COCKTAIL PARTY

PENTACLE

Project Name

5 Close out (and hand over to process) to ensure that after the benefits effort the benefits are gained

How will you test that the success criteria have been achieved?

How will you ensure that the benefits continue to be gained?

How will you carry out your post implementation review?

What other project specific issues do you have to deal with?

TRUMPCARDS™

Pocket-sized Prompts

I made these for you to cut out and carry around. I hope they help.

eo

Perfect Project TrumpCard ™

Laws of change

1. One change leads to another
2. Adding change to change creates chaos
3. People create change - People constrain change

Success Formula

$$\left(\frac{(P,C/PT*L\&R) +P\&C +SHM}{T} \right) * L \;=\; \text{Success}$$

Change matched to project type managed through effective learning and review plus planning and co-ordination plus effective stakeholder management shared amongst the team multiplied by effective leadership

Dr. Eddie Obeng

Resources

Website - pentaclethevbs.com
Change Club - allchange.com
Project Healthcheck -
pentaclethevbs.com/healthchecks.htm
Email - eddie_obeng@pentaclethevbs.com

1/6

WWW.PENTACLE.CO.UK   EMAIL: EDDIE_OBENG@PENTACLETHE VBS.COM

Purpose, Change & Project type TrumpCard ™

Always	Never
• Know why the change is being carried out.	• Ignore the project type.
• Chunk the change in to early effort- early benefit.	• Do a V.
• Decide what type of project it is.	• Ignore the effect of 'visibility' and driver/ deliverer.
• Know the balance between fast, cheap, and good.	• Run a project which doesn't help the Money Making Machine.
• Use the right method for the type of project.	• Forget the people who will have to live with your project.

Remember:

• Bubble diagram or Gap analysis
• Chunk it or Junk it!
• 4 Project types Fog, Paint-by- numbers, Quest, Movie

2/6

PENTACLE

WWW.PENTACLE.CO.UK   EMAIL: EDDIE_OBENG@PENTACLETHE VBS.COM

Stakeholder Management TrumpCard™

Always	Never
•Know who they are.	•Ignore them.
•Get them emotionally engaged.	•Make assumptions on their behalf - test instead.
•Map them.	•Surprise them.
•Communicate <frequency/ method>.	•Let expectations go out of balance with reality.
•Agree ground rules for working together & close loops.	•Ignore their success criteria (hard/soft).

Remember:

- •Dead body syndrome
- •Anxiety gap
- •Understand - Agree grid

3/6

PENTACLE

WWW.PENTACLE.CO.UK   EMAIL: EDDIE_OBENG@PENTACLETH EVBS.COM

Planning, Risk & Co-ordination TrumpCard™

Always	Never
•Gain & share perspective with your stakeholders.	•Ask, 'Do you understand?'
•Think about the future impact.	•Ignore a risk, wait for it to go wrong and then say 'I knew that was going to happen'!
•Identify risks, plan how you will eliminate, keep an eye on them, or neutralise them.	•Use the wrong level of communication.
	•Try to do it all yourself.
•Set realistic timescales.	•Leave it until you are already late before you start to communicate.
•Schedule communication.	

Remember:

- •Sticky steps
- •Hopes & Fears
- •Communication plan
- •Emotion/Complexity scale

4/6

PENTACLE

Leadership and Team Development TrumpCard™

Always	Never
•Lead - choose the best behaviour to match.	•Use 'Love me as I am..'
•Monitor the team mood.	•Ignore team issues.
•Create the best mix of team behaviours for your type of project.	•Stop developing and building the team.
	•Take sides.
	•Lose your focus on the soft success criteria.
•Use the project leader's question.	•Treat everyone the same.
•Use responsibility matrices.	•Show that you don't believe in the goal.

Remember:
•Circle of inclusion
•Doers, Carers, Solvers, Knowers, Checkers - Compensating actions
•Adapter, Pioneer, Innovator, Craftsman - behaviour check

5/6

Learning and Review
TrumpCard™

Always

- Have a review when you are at your most busy.
- Actively communicate when the scope changes.
- Capture and repeat your learnings.
- Check where people are on the learning curve.
- Plan it in as an action.

Never

- Make people feel threatened.
- Focus exclusively on past passive events.
- Respond to lateness by throwing more resource at the late part.
- Skip steps on the journey from experience through reflection to theory to planning to test.
- Cancel reviews.

Remember:

- Here to There diagram
- Action replay
- Comms plan
- Emotion/Complexity scale

6/6

WWW.PENTACLE.CO.UK   EMAIL: EDDIE_OBENG@PENTACLETH EVBS.COM

FURTHER COACHING AND LEARNING

The advantage of owning a Virtual Business School is that you can provide interesting and different services which people can experience and use locally at home or in their offices - even on a transatlantic flight!

I hope you get some value out of my suggestions.

eo

PROJECT MANAGER'S PHONE HELP-LINE

Pentacle VoiceWorks provides a phone help-line for project managers. You can access this by checking the phone number on PentacleTheVBS.com/PerfectProjects.htm If you pass the test and join allchange.com you will also get updates on new topics and services.

PERFECT PROJECTS MASTERCLASS

We design and run Perfect Projects masterclasses for project managers from a single organisation. You can find more information at PentacleTheVBS.com/ppmasterclass.htm

ON-LINE E-CLUBS

Pentacle runs a number of on-line clubs for people with different areas of interest. The one most relevant for you will be allchange.com – you can subscribe on a monthly basis but to get in you'll have to pass a short test. You can take your test at PentacleTheVBS.com/actest.htm

BOOKS, POSTERS, MATERIALS

If you want to learn more about my New World approach you can read the other books in the New World library.

Other books by Eddie Obeng in the New World Library:

 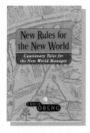  

E-mail us for information

Perfect.Projects@PentacleTheVBS.com

SPECIAL OFFER

For a 10% discount on copies of *All Change!* purchased from Pentacle Works, cut out and post this coupon with your order to:

Pentacle Works
Burke Lodge, 20 London End, Beaconsfield, Bucks HP9 2JH

Subject to availability and company discretion

Index